# BUY & SELL RECREATIONAL PROPERTY IN CANADA

# BUY & SELL RECREATIONAL PROPERTY IN CANADA

Geraldine Santiago, Realtor

**Self-Counsel Press**
*(a division of)*
International Self-Counsel Press Ltd.
Canada     USA

*Self-Counsel Press acknowledges the financial support of the Government of Canada through the Book Publishing Industry Development Program (BPIDP) for our publishing activities.*

*Printed in Canada*

*First edition: 2006*

**Library and Archives Canada Cataloguing in Publication**

Santiago, Geraldine
    Buy & sell recreational property in Canada / Geraldine Santiago.

    (Self-counsel reference series)
    ISBN-10: 1-55180-693-2
    ISBN-13: 978-1-55180-693-8

    1. Second homes.  2. House buying.  3. House selling.
I. Title.  II. Title: Buy and sell recreational property in Canada.
III. Series.
HD1379.S258 2006     643'.25     C2006-902097-3

**Self-Counsel Press**
*(a division of)*
International Self-Counsel Press Ltd.

| 1481 Charlotte Road | 1704 North State Street |
| North Vancouver, BC  V7J 1H1 | Bellingham, WA  98225 |
| Canada | USA |

# CONTENTS

# NOTICE TO READERS

The author, publisher, and the vendor of this book make no representations or warranties regarding the outcome or the use to which the information in this book is put and are not assuming any liability for any claims, losses, or damages arising out of the use of this book. The reader should not rely on the author or publisher of this book for any professional advice. Please be sure that you have the most recent edition.

# ACKNOWLEDGEMENTS

I gratefully acknowledge the important contributions made by other people in writing this book.

I would like to thank all the agents throughout Canada who provided me with information on the recreational market in their local areas.

I wish to thank Tanya Howe for her hard work, insight, and dedication. I wish to thank Richard Day at Self-Counsel Press for giving me the opportunity to write this book, Barbara Kuhne for overseeing its editing, and everyone at Self-Counsel Press who has helped to make this book a success.

Last, but not least, thank you to my husband, David, and my two daughters, Luisa and Lauren, for their continued support and encouragement.

# INTRODUCTION

Since the early part of 2000, recreational property sales across Canada have increased, and trends are showing that this will continue for some time. Major influences that have given rise to increased sales in recreational property include interest rates at a 40-year low and increased consumer confidence and job security. These factors have led to increased demand for recreational property, particularly near greater metropolitan areas.

First-time recreational-home purchasers should do their homework carefully. Compared to purchasing property in the city or suburbs, there are many more factors to consider when purchasing recreational property. These factors vary and are often unique to specific regions, provinces, and municipalities. Buyers need to educate themselves about bylaws unique to each municipality, as well as provincial and federal regulations that pertain to fisheries, oceans, wildlife, forests, and the environment. Environmental considerations with regard to real estate

typically fall under a provincial department of the environment or a ministry of natural resources. Should you wish to alter or make additions to your recreational property near or on water, there could also be federal laws that affect and restrict your intended use of the property.

This book provides basic information for buyers and sellers of recreational homes, in the hope that your recreational-home purchase or sale will be a satisfying and rewarding experience.

## What Do You Need to Know about the Recreational Housing Market?

Before purchasing or selling your recreational home, it is important to look at larger market conditions, such as local and national housing prices, mortgage rates, and the amount of new home construction underway. The Canada Mortgage and Housing Corporation (CMHC) Market Analysis Centre assists home buyers and sellers to understand how the housing market is evolving. This resource regularly publishes local market analysis reports and provides information on recent trends in housing market conditions. Your local CMHC market analyst can also tell you if there is currently a buyer's market, a seller's market, or a balanced housing market in the area you are interested in.

## Buyer's market

In a buyer's market, the number of recreational homes available for sale exceeds the demand, so prices either stabilize or drop. With fewer buyers and more homes, not only do you as the buyer have more options to choose from, but you also have more negotiating leverage. You have more time to look for the right home, and you can evaluate the choices without feeling pressure to act quickly.

## Seller's market

In a seller's market, the seller dictates the price. The number of buyers exceeds the number of properties for sale. In this situation of low inventory, a seller often gets his or her asking price — and sometimes more — because there may be a bidding war in which there are competing or multiple offers.

## Balanced market

In a balanced market, there are approximately an equal number of buyers and sellers. If you are a buyer in this market, you will probably not have to go through bidding wars because there are enough recreational properties listed on the market.

## Supply and demand

Demand for recreational real estate has already exceeded supply in many areas throughout Canada. Contributing factors are low interest rates, more international buyers, baby boomers reaching retirement age, and a decreasing number of waterfront properties. As a result, the demand for less traditional recreational properties has increased. In many markets, small farms and acreage sales are on the upswing. Also growing in popularity are leasehold properties. In many cases, purchasers of leases (of up to 99 years) are permitted to tear down existing buildings and build to their specifications on the land. (See Chapter 2 for more information about leasehold property.)

# Who Is Buying Recreational Property in Canada?

Baby boomers, empty nesters, and retirees are the primary demographic that is buying recreational properties from coast to coast. Many buyers are between the ages of 40 to 60. Many of them can afford a recreational home because they have enjoyed business success or have inherited family money. As well, many Americans, Europeans, Australians, and Asians are attracted to recreational properties in Canada. The impetus to buy recreational real estate is primarily twofold: for personal pleasure and as an investment whose value will increase over time.

# What Are Buyers Paying for Recreational Properties?

According to a recent report that covers more than 40 markets from Salt Spring Island, British Columbia, to Shediac Bay, New Brunswick, sales and prices have been increasing over recent years in most markets across the country.

Cottage prices have increased significantly, year after year. Because of uncertainty due to political turmoil around the world, many people are opting to stay closer to home rather than travel abroad. This has had an impact on recreational-property buyers. For example, most purchasers in Newfoundland are from St. John's and its surrounding communities, and again, they are baby boomers — people with equity in their homes and a double income.

The following sections outline some of the popular regions and the price ranges for recreational properties across Canada.

## British Columbia

On British Columbia's Sunshine Coast, the starting price for a three-bedroom winterized recreational property on a standard-sized waterfront lot can range from $300,000 to $500,000. For the same style of property in the South Cariboo region, the starting price is $200,000, and on Harrison Lake it is $425,000.

Other areas of interest in BC are Whistler and Salt Spring Island, where many properties cost more than $1 million. Americans, Albertans, and to a lesser extent Europeans and Australians are purchasing here. In the Okanagan Valley, in BC's interior, prices are more reasonable, starting at $200,000.

At the Sun Peaks Resort in southern BC, the market remains well balanced with supply meeting demand. But prices have increased year after year, with a two-bedroom ski-in/ski-out condominium starting at $300,000. Out of town purchasers are from Calgary and Edmonton as well as from the US and the UK.

## Alberta

West of Edmonton the starting price for a three-bedroom winterized recreational property on a standard-sized waterfront lot is $175,000. In Sylvan Lake in central Alberta, the starting price is $520,000, although waterfront properties can reach $750,000.

## Saskatchewan

In Prince Albert, Saskatchewan, the starting price for a three-bedroom winterized recreational property on the lakefront is $250,000. It is a seller's market all around with low inventory and high demand for such properties.

## Manitoba

In the eastern part of Manitoba, prices vary from $100,000 for a simple cottage to $645,000 for a two-bedroom customized waterfront home on Lac Du Bonnet.

## Ontario

In Ontario, huge price tags are not uncommon; in some areas recreational homes can range from $1 million to $6 million. In Grand Bend, at the southwestern end of Lake Huron, the starting price is $400,000 and in the Muskoka Lakes region the starting price is $450,000.

## Quebec

In Quebec, recreational buyers are most active in the Laurentians (north of Montreal) and in the Eastern Townships. The Laurentian real estate business has been booming ever since Intrawest invested more than $1 billion in various infrastructure projects to attract the baby-boomer market to Mont Tremblant. With its European style architecture, this resort is a condominium paradise for the pre-retired and "active retired" who can afford the lifestyle. This unique holiday spot has become the strongest economic player north of the Montreal metropolitan area.

The attraction towards the Eastern Townships is another story. This is one of the oldest regions in Canada, and you can still buy houses that were built during the Loyalist era in the 1800s. Buyers are attracted to the scenic views, particularly around Sutton, Dunham, Frelighsburg, and Brome Lake.

The Brome Lake (Knowlton) area is famous for attracting top buyers from Montreal and farther away. Prices start at $300,000 for a simple cottage, but the sky is the limit if you want a premium lakefront spot or acreage with a view.

Both of these Quebec regions are attracting weekenders and baby boomers, though nowadays Mont Tremblant is also attracting more and more European tourists.

## Nova Scotia

A two-bedroom recreational cottage on lake-front property in Lunenburg, on Nova Scotia's south shore, starts at $158,000, and oceanfront prices soar to $1 million.

In Big Bras D'or on Cape Breton Island, prices for a recreational cottage with accessible waterfront start at $225,000. At a 30-minute drive from Yarmouth, you will find waterfront cottage properties starting at $300,000.

## New Brunswick

In Shediac Bay, New Brunswick, recreational properties start at $150,000. It remains a seller's market in part because with low interest rates, many baby boomers are purchasing recreational properties. One factor that is limiting the number of available properties is that many families are handing their recreational properties down from one generation to the next. Recreational property in the Northumberland Straight area starts at $600,000. Canadians, Americans, Britons, and Europeans are attracted to the area's reasonably priced land.

## Prince Edward Island

Once the best-kept secret for recreational property, Prince Edward Island is gaining in popularity. Currently, a waterfront property starts at $200,000. In PEI, buyers from the United States, Canada, and Europe drive recreational property sales. The external demand has exerted pressure on cottage prices and is making the market less affordable for local residents.

Note that Prince Edward Island imposes ownership restrictions that limit beachfront property to 165 feet. This prevents international developers from monopolizing beachfront properties.

## Newfoundland and Labrador

In Newfoundland and Labrador, low interest rates coupled with a shortage of listings have created a seller's market. Buyers are primarily from out of province and the United States. In Newtown, in central Newfoundland, a three-bedroom oceanfront property, though extremely rare, is valued at approximately $100,000; in Humber Valley, prices can reach $1 million.

## The Yukon

Fishing, hunting, skiing (both downhill and cross-country), hiking, rockhounding, kayaking/canoeing, boating, snowmobiling, and horseback riding are all popular activities in the Yukon, and these outdoor sports encourage recreational-property sales.

Popular recreational areas in and around Whitehorse are the southern lakes, in particular Marsh Lake and Tagish Lake, and north of Whitehorse, Lake Laberge and Fox Lake. It is currently a seller's market, with waterfront property in high demand. Prices range from $100,000 for a cabin that needs to be fixed up, to $500,000 for a luxury cottage with great views. For recreational property not located on waterfront, there is a balanced market, with prices starting at $80,000.

## The Northwest Territories

Activities such as trout lake fishing and snow-mobiling contribute to the popularity of this northern area for recreational users. Since 2003, in parts of the Northwest Territories there has been a seller's market, influenced in part by an influx of new workers building pipelines and working in diamond mines. Cabins in Tibbit Lake, near Yellowknife, start at $60,000, but many properties in this area are located on leased land. Road access during the winter may also be difficult.

# Cottage Associations of Canada

Cottage associations exist to help cottage owners who have cottage-related problems or questions. A cottage association can be an invaluable resource when you are buying or selling a recreational property. Some associations include real estate sections on their websites, while others may post only upcoming community activities. Cottagers' associations can also help in other areas. For example, Ontario cottagers' associations recently had input into the public consultation process that led to a land claims settlement with the Wahta Mohawk. See the appendix for a list of cottage associations.

# A Note about Terminology

If you are new to buying or selling real estate or unfamiliar with some of the commonly used terms, please consult the glossary for definitions. Note that the terms "real estate agent" and "agent" are used interchangeably in this book.

# PART 1
## PREPARING TO BUY
## RECREATIONAL PROPERTY

# Chapter 1

# SEARCHING FOR THAT PERFECT RECREATIONAL HOME

There are many options available to recreational home and property purchasers. You must consider your preferences for location and lifestyle. Couples or partners purchasing a recreational home together may need to make compromises or trade-offs. Choosing the right recreational home for you and deciding which areas best suit your needs are very personal choices.

Assess your personal preferences and think about the kind of lifestyle change living on a recreational property would entail, even if it's for short vacations. For most people, a recreational home does not necessarily translate to living in a rustic log cabin in the thick of the woods. Rather, their ideal recreational home may have all the comforts of home, including custom cabinetry, spacious master suites, a gourmet kitchen, a home theatre system, specialty flooring, nine-foot ceilings, a landscaped backyard, a games room, and more. As a first time recreational purchaser, you need to think about what kind of needs and expectations you have (and determine how unrealistic some of these expectations may be!).

## Where Do You Start?

Start looking for recreational real estate properties by scanning classified advertisements, Internet websites, and local real estate magazines. Multiple Listing Service (MLS), put out by the Canadian Real Estate Association, contains in-depth details of properties and is a valuable resource. An MLS feature sheet can contain information such as —

- price;
- total area;
- previous year's taxes;
- monthly charges pertaining to strata title ownership;
- distance to schools;
- distance to transportation services;
- parking facilities (e.g., garage, multiple car park);
- outdoor areas such as a large lot, balcony, patio, and/or sundeck;

- geographical features, and views from the property;
- nearby recreation centres and/or fitness centres;
- central location;
- type and number of fireplaces;
- swimming pool, hot tub, and/or sauna; and
- library and/or games room.

The MLS feature sheet is a very important document because potential buyers rely on the accuracy of the information. The information is included in a computerized data system to which the real estate board in your area contributes. The list can be obtained from the local board, from your realtor, or by browsing www.mls.ca or www.realtylink.org.

Note that the MLS does not include "For Sale by Owner" (FSBO) properties on its website. Only properties listed by an agent are included. (See the section Homes for Sale by Owner later on in this chapter, as well as Chapter 16, for more information on FSBOs.)

# Factors to Consider When Looking for a Recreational Home

Location, location, location! When searching for your recreational property, think about your and your family's lifestyle needs. Some things to consider: the type of community and neighbourhood, privacy, preferred activities, accessibility, seasons and climate, strata restrictions, zoning and developments, and home warranty.

## Community

Most cottage buyers base their decisions on price, but lifestyle requirements are equally important. Younger couples, for example, often want to be close to a small community where they and their children can enjoy community events and programs.

Recreational home purchasers who are semi-retired or retired may want a more peaceful and tranquil setting, away from the noise and hustle and bustle of a community, and perhaps closer to a golf course or a beach.

## Neighbourhood

When considering the neighbourhood you want, look at the area surrounding your recreational home. Are the neighbours similar to you? Are they young couples, families with teenage children, or retired couples?

Talk to the residents in the neighbourhood, and walk around the area to get a better sense of the community. You may want to find out about the local politics: Do the locals resent the number of city people who are buying property for seasonal use? Are there strong views from the locals about whether to allow more density as more recreational buyers move into the neighbourhood? Will you spend enough time in the community to be affected by local political differences?

Consider potential pollutants in your chosen neighbourhood. Noise pollution may be caused by highways, industry, or airports; odour pollution may result from farms or industry; and chemical pollution may come from farms, industry, or even golf courses (which are maintained using pesticides, herbicides, and fertilizers).

You may find the quality and availability of municipal services important, such as hospitals, police and fire departments, road maintenance, garbage collection, mail delivery, and snow removal. Make sure that you understand what services the neighbourhood has to offer and whether or not they are suited to your needs.

## Privacy

When buying recreational property — whether it is a one-acre property or a 20-acre property — many people want or need privacy from their neighbours, or from the world in general. Different types of fences can be used to obtain privacy, including chain-link fences, wooden fences, or trees along the border of a property. It is important for owners of recreational property to realize that although they have a variety of ways to obtain privacy, they may not block off access roads, rights-of-ways, and so on.

## Preferred activities

What activities you prefer to participate in should also be considered when purchasing your recreational home. What do you plan to do on your property? If you plan to raise horses or farm worms, is this permitted? Are you allowed to fish or hunt on your property? Note that fishing is strictly regulated by each province and you do require a licence to fish on your property. Before making any plans to fish, contact the provincial government for current regulations.

## Accessibility

Few city dwellers concern themselves with getting around by car. The situation is quite the opposite for many recreational homeowners. The nearest public highway cannot always be accessed from the local public road; sometimes it can only be accessed via a private road. You must investigate whether the access is public or private and whether there is a restrictive covenant on title (see Chapter 6 for more information). You may also want to consider who is responsible for the upkeep of the access or roadway and whether it is open year-round.

In some situations, the cottage may be on an island and accessible only by water. Provisions must be made for water transport as well as parking facilities on the mainland.

Accessibility to your recreational home is very important for many reasons. One thing to consider is resale value: usually, people living in the city want a very short distance to get to their recreational property, with minimal commuting hassles.

Equally important is access in and around the area where you purchase. For example, some waterfront cottages can only be accessed by water taxi, and this can increase your vacation expenses. If your getaway can only be accessed by way of a water taxi, seaplane, train, or ferry — or perhaps a combination of these — think of the cost of each of these transportation methods as this will add to your cost of owning a recreational property, especially if you were to commute on a regular basis. Also, you will need to consider the costs of transporting supplies and materials if you were to fix, renovate, or build on your property.

## Seasonal or year-round property

Is the area in which you are planning to purchase ideal for year-round activities or only for seasonal activities? If you owned a recreational home in British Columbia's Okanagan Valley, for example, you could enjoy swimming, boating, and waterskiing in the summer, skiing in the winter, and wine festivals throughout most of the year. This provides the recreational-home owner with maximum enjoyment of the property.

If you intend to use your property year-round, you should be looking for a property that is winterized — property that can be used and occupied during the winter period. Non-winterized properties need to be prepared for vacancy during winter months. For example, waterlines must be drained and water supply shut off.

## Maintenance

Maintenance is always a concern, especially if you do not spend time on the property year-round and you have not hired an in-house caretaker. You may want to find out if you can hire the assistance of a local caretaker who will work on a weekly or monthly basis to ensure that your home remains secure and undamaged. Sometimes, you will find your neighbours in the same or similar situation, in which case you can perhaps hire a caretaker together. Another option is to have a system in which your neighbours check your recreational home when you are not vacationing there, and vice versa.

Perhaps there is a local recreational homeowners' association or cottage owners' association where a caretaker or a property manager of some sort is already hired. Contact the association in your area and find out what your options are.

Another option is to rent out the property, either directly or through a rental company. More and more rental companies specializing in resort-type recreational properties not only offer property management services, but will take care of everything from marketing and booking guests for your property to cleaning and dealing with emergencies. In any type of rental activity, there will be some risk of damage to your property, so make sure that you have the proper documentation, insurance, and permits to allow for renting.

## Strata or condominium restrictions

Buying a condominium involves a type of housing ownership that is more formally known as strata title ownership. In addition to ownership of a unit, you share ownership of common areas, such as hallways, garages, and elevators, and share financial responsibility for their maintenance with the other owners of the building. This is reflected in monthly maintenance charges.

If you are interested in purchasing a property such as a condominium, find out about the bylaws and other rules that govern that property. You may also want to ask for documentation on the history of the property and include, in your offer to purchase, a statement that you are satisfied with the disclosure statement that the seller has provided. (Property condition disclosure statements are discussed in Chapters 11 and 15).

Restrictions vary from one housing development to another. Find out what the restrictions are and whether there are strata corporation bylaws, rules, or regulations that impose restrictions or prohibitions. It is very helpful to obtain strata council meeting minutes going back as far as possible — at least for the past 12 months — and including the most recent annual general meeting.

Common restrictions include age restrictions, which, for example, specify that some developments are designated for adult-only residents; rental restrictions, which limit the number of residential strata units that can be rented; and restrictions on the size, weight, number, and type of pets. Restrictions are not necessarily a negative issue for homebuyers. For example, although there may be restrictions that limit or prohibit rentals, this may be a positive factor for buyers, in that most or all the occupiers of a building are also owners.

Most strata corporations also place restrictions on the following:

- "Use" — specifying what activities cannot take place on the property (such as running a business)

- Window coverings — imposing uniformity of colour of window coverings

- Waterbeds — prohibiting, requiring damage insurance, or restricting their location within the building

- Hot tubs — prohibiting placement on roof decks because of potential damage from leaks or weight

- Hardwood floors — prohibiting them because of noise, especially in frame buildings

## Zoning

Under the authority of the municipal government, zoning specifies the types of buildings that may be built on particular properties and how those buildings may be used: as residential property (a single-family unit, a multi-family unit, and/or a duplex), as recreational property, or as a commercial or industrial building. Look for zoning information on your MLS feature sheet. Ask about the zoning of surrounding properties to determine if, for example, a factory or condominium development might suddenly appear nearby. Also be aware of the possibility of zoning changes in the future. If you purchase a home with a view, for example, check to see if that view is legally protected. Find out whether there are height restrictions that will keep someone from erecting a building that will block your view.

## Zoning and developments

Zoning in areas where there are recreational properties differs significantly from zoning in a more established community or city. Most homes in a city are found in subdivisions. There are highly developed city plans, and residences are developed in predictable patterns. Lots are usually based upon subdivision agreements registered on the title of the property. These agreements set out the pattern of the building, confirm water, sewage, and other utilities, and establish the layout of roadways, sidewalks, and parks.

Cottage developments rarely follow a predictable pattern or plan. Cottage properties that border waterfronts have often been subdivided over the course of many years. Development in the area may be sporadic. In many cases, municipal involvement is kept to a minimum and most of the day-to-day concerns are handled by cottage associations.

Some municipalities in cottage country have passed seasonal zoning provisions. This could very well prevent the conversion of a cottage into a year-round recreational property or retirement home. If this is in your plans, be sure to verify the zoning bylaws (or ask your realtor to verify them for you). Plans for expansion or winterization may be futile. Without being able to use the cottage year-round, the cottage's marketability can be adversely affected.

## Zoning restrictions on rentals

If the recreational home is not your primary residence and you are planning to use it only for limited periods of time, you may wish to consider renting your recreational home to generate extra income. This income can help pay down your mortgage or contribute to costs of maintenance, utilities, insurance, and so on.

However, you must be aware that district bylaws vary from municipality to municipality. For example, in a resort community properties can be located in several different zones. This could mean that some properties are located in zones that allow for both residential and tourism use, while other areas do not allow rental periods that are less than 28 consecutive days because that is considered tourist accommodation and is not allowed in some residential zones.

Some regions don't specify rental periods in their zoning bylaws. In some areas where tourism is promoted (for example, in areas near a ski resort) daily rentals are allowed. Some recreational properties are purchased solely to provide rental accommodation.

In some areas there are no formal restrictions on short-term rentals; however, bylaws are subject to change. Make sure that you know what the municipal bylaws and zoning restrictions are pertaining to your property.

## New-home warranties

There are pros and cons to consider when deciding whether to buy a new recreational home or a resale. Buying a new recreational home means that you may be able to choose or upgrade the finishing materials, flooring, cabinets, and electrical features. As well, the building will comply with the latest building and electrical codes and energy-efficiency standards, which will result in lower maintenance costs.

But more important, recreational home-buyers may want the security of new-home warranty programs that are available in most provinces. Contact a new-home warranty office or visit its website for a list of registered builders in the area where you are considering purchasing. Although warranty coverage varies from one province to another, typically the programs guarantee labour and materials for your new home for at least one year after completion. The warranty also ensures that major structural defects will be corrected for a minimum of five years (and up to ten years in some provinces).

At present, warranties are required by law in Ontario, Quebec, and British Columbia, and are voluntary in most other provinces. In British Columbia, the law requires consumer coverage to be provided in the form of home warranty insurance, which is a bona fide insurance product that can only be sold by government-approved insurance companies.

Comprehensive warranties on newly built recreational homes are readily available and easily obtained. Even in provinces where the warranty is not mandatory, many lenders will not grant you a mortgage unless you obtain a warranty. Clearly, a warranty is a good thing to get, as it offers you peace of mind.

# Homes Directly for Sale by the Owner

Sometimes you will find that a recreational property you are interested in is being sold by the owner, as a "For Sale by Owner" (FSBO, pronounced "fizbo"), usually because the seller wants to save on agents' fees. You should be aware of the advantages and disadvantages of purchasing a FSBO.

First, FSBOs tend to be priced according to what the owner would like the homes to sell for, rather than what the market is willing to pay. If you are looking at various types of properties, including FSBO properties, make sure that your agent provides you with a comparative market analysis (CMA) to verify if the price is within fair market value.

Second, it is common practice for sellers to hire the services of a listing agent. The listing agent has a code of ethics to which he or she is bound. He or she is also bound by the laws of the country and has a fiduciary duty to inform his or her client who is selling a property about the legal importance of full disclosure. It is also the listing agent's responsibility to verify the accuracy of the information being given to the potential buyer. Not having an agent working on behalf of the seller may raise questions regarding the disclosure of water damage, mould problems, and other serious health and safety issues.

Buyers' agents, in seeing that there is no listing agent to represent the seller, may find purchasing a FSBO a potential risk because there may not be any confirmation about the history of the property or the accuracy of what is disclosed. A buyer's agent has a fiduciary duty to protect the client's interests, and the seller of a FSBO may not be aware of his or her duty as an owner to disclose all information. So, if you are buying a recreational property for the first time, retain a buyer's agent to ensure that your interests are protected at all times.

There are perhaps only two reasons for purchasing a FSBO. First, both parties can save on agents' fees because there is no commission to be paid. This may influence both parties in coming to an agreed-to price, which may or may not be lower than fair market value. Second, a bidding war is unlikely to happen. Because the property is not listed on the MLS, the chances of people finding out about it (unless it is very well advertised) are reduced. Go to the following websites for more information regarding FSBOs:

- www.fsbo.ca
- www.homesellcanada.com
- www.forsalebyowner.com (US website)

# Chapter 2
# TYPES OF RECREATIONAL PROPERTIES AND TYPES OF OWNERSHIP

There are many different types of recreational housing structures, and determining which is right for you will largely depend on your lifestyle, your budget, and how you would like to use your property. Recreational-home purchasers need to determine exactly what their needs and desires are, as there are many possibilities — for example, a chalet at a ski resort, a floating home on a lake, a log cabin in a forest, or a mobile or manufactured home in a new development. Each housing structure has its positive and negative qualities. You may not find something that meets all of your expectations; some compromises may become necessary.

## Cottages and Summer Cabins

What do you want your cottage or summer cabin to be like? Would you like a small, cozy cottage that comfortably fits two people — or a big summer cabin that fits 12? You can find a rustic cabin with an outhouse and an old wood stove, or you can find one with large picture windows looking out onto the lake, with electricity, hot and cold running water, satellite TV, and all the comforts of a residential home.

When you are considering buying a property for seasonal use, you will need to factor in the costs and arrangements for security and maintenance during the off-season — for example, if it is only to be used during the summer. Ask your neighbours or those in a similar situation what type of arrangements they make. Perhaps your cottage is in a development that already provides year-round security guards patrolling the neighbourhood on a regular basis, and perhaps there is a cottage association that has a management company that will take care of your maintenance needs.

## Floating Homes

A floating home is a special type of houseboat without a motor. If you are considering purchasing a floating home, it must be sold in conjunction with a water lot in order to qualify as real estate. Without an attachment to land, however, it remains simply a "boat," which is considered a chattel — and agents are prohibited from selling chattels.

Most water lots are leased but some allow for private ownership, sometimes called "fee-simple ownership," which means the owner has the right to control, use, and transfer the property. Water lots are usually divided into strata-titled units, and they are registered in the land registry office.

Many floating-home owners would say that aside from the sheer beauty of living on the water, the lack of yard work (such as mowing the lawn or trimming hedges) and the close ties that develop within the floating-home community are some of the benefits.

A problem you may find when considering buying a floating home is that many financial institutions are reluctant to give a mortgage for this style of housing because it is still perceived as unconventional. There are also monthly marina fees to consider, which help pay for dock maintenance and services such as sewage and water.

When considering purchasing a floating home, it is important to conduct due diligence as there may be issues that are different from purchasing a recreational home on land. Many floating homes are located in a floating-home community, such as one found in a marina. Most of these communities already have water and sewage connections established. There may also be covered parking lots included with the price, or a garage nearby where you can park your vehicle.

You may also want to consider the unique maintenance costs for your floating home. In some areas you may find it difficult or expensive to find someone with the specialized skills for dealing with floating-home maintenance, while in other areas the marina will offer the services of experienced carpenters, electricians, plumbers, and so on.

Typically, each marina has its own separate contract, terms, conditions, and/or lease agreement for you to sign. Take the time to read the fine print carefully. There are many complicated issues that you should be aware of, such as what types of amenities are included, the cost of association fees, available moorage, etc. Equally important are site development standards, spacing, resident access, water supply, sewage disposal, solid waste collection and disposal, rodent and insect control, electrical power, and general safety. There may also be restrictions for the type of floating home allowed in the marina, such as height, design, dimensions, and internal layout.

If you are considering building your own floating home, there are architectural standards to take into account. For example, floating homes need to be both fireproof and unsinkable, and in many communities they cannot exceed three storeys in height. Professional help is required as floating homes are an engineering specialty. You may need to contact the local chapter of the National Association of Marine Surveyors (NAMS), or the Professional Engineers Association of your province. You may also want to read the Canada Marine Act for more information.

## Condominiums

If you buy a condominium, you will be governed by that property's bylaws and regulations. Before you buy, read the minutes of the condominium's strata council meetings, and find out the rules and regulations that the strata council has established.

When purchasing a condominium, be aware that some areas, such as Whistler, BC, have "unrestricted" and "restricted" classifications for condominiums. An unrestricted unit, also known as a "Phase One" condo, is generally found in the small, lodge-type buildings in the village. There are no restrictions on owner usage, but an organized rental program is available for those times when the owner is not using the unit. An example of an organized rental program is one in which the developer, management company, strata corporation, or group of owners has hired a property management company to look after the rental of the entire condominium's units, handling bookings, cleaning, maintenance, and so on.

A restricted unit is also known as a "Phase Two" condo. These are studio and one- and two-bedroom apartment condominiums incorporated into a resort hotel. The owner is restricted to occupying the unit for 28 days in the winter and 28 days in the summer. Benefits of buying a Phase Two condo include revenue from renting your allotted time in the unit, a potential tax shelter, and access to various hotel services and facilities during one's stay. This type of unit is best suited for the occasional visitor to Whistler or for the investor only interested in revenue.

You should speak to a qualified agent in the area who can provide you with more details about these types of restrictions and uses.

## Ski-in/Ski-out Condominiums

Ski-in/ski-out condominiums mean that you can literally ski in and ski out of the door of your property! It is important to find out whether the property you are purchasing is truly a ski-in/ski-out condominium. Although there are many properties advertised as "ski-in/ski-out," a ski hill may still be quite a distance from the property.

Sometimes ski resorts have a central ski village where restaurants, pubs, and ski repair shops are located. It may be that the central ski village is located far from the property and that you need to drive to get to the village centre.

If you do purchase a true ski-in/ski-out property, it is a very good investment. If you choose to rent out your property, it is obviously very desirable for vacation skiers; and if you choose to sell, the resale value is very high.

## Ski Chalets and Winter Cabins

When purchasing a ski chalet or winter cabin it is most likely that you will be purchasing in a developed area that offers a multitude of activities for the entire family, such as snowboarding, skating, skiing (downhill and cross-country), snowmobiling, ice fishing, and snowshoeing. Consider the location of the property. How close is it to these activities, the ski village, or the lake for ice fishing? How close are the amenities?

There are many "dream homes" in developed ski areas. Many winter cabins are state-of-the-art log cabins that are rainproof and durable as well as eco-friendly. Such winter cabins may also have skylight windows, fireplaces, hot tubs, and many other luxury features.

If you are purchasing in a ski resort, find out what types of security are available for the area, but more specifically for your property. This becomes more of an issue should you be away for extended periods of time. Keep in mind that many ski resort developments offer security patrol for the community. You may also want to ask your agent about road clearing services during heavy winter snowfalls.

## Mobile Homes, Mobile-Home Parks, and Land-Lease Communities

Mobile homes, or "RVs," can be broadly defined as portable residential units that can be transported by a towing device, used as a place to live while travelling or on vacation, but sometimes also as a permanent dwelling. A mobile-home park is a residential area that is composed of two or more mobile homes. A landlord provides the land as well as the services and facilities. A land-lease community is similar to a mobile-home park, except that the homes are more permanent structures.

Provincial tenancy acts (in Ontario it is called the Tenant Protection Act) cover landlord and tenant relations in a mobile-home park or land-lease community only if the tenant owns the dwelling in which he or she lives, and if the dwelling is used as the permanent residence of the occupant. In cases where the mobile home is not the permanent residence, disputes between landlords and tenants can be brought to an independent agency such as the Ontario Rental Housing Tribunal.

Real estate agents are increasingly involved with mobile and land-lease homes as a result of the aging Canadian population as well as pricing advantages that are associated with land leases. In mobile-home parks and land-lease communities, the landlord retains possession of the land, the facilities, and the services designed for the common use and enjoyment of the tenants.

Ask your agent for information regarding land leases if you are considering entering into such an agreement.

# Hunting Cabins

Hunting and fishing are specialized sports, and if you are purchasing a hunting cabin for these purposes, there is a lot to find out about the property and all that it has to offer. Find out what type of wildlife and/or fish can be caught nearby. Different areas may have an assortment of wildlife, but may not have exactly the type of wildlife you prefer to hunt. Are there moose, bears, white-tailed deer, grouse, and/or turkey? What is the nearest body or bodies of water, and what kind of fishing is available?

Hunting cabins tend to be more rustic, and the normal comforts of home may or may not be included. Ask to see what exactly is included with the price, such as propane lights, propane tanks, gasoline generators, storage batteries, and so on. Some cabins may even include canoes, motorboats, or camping gear with the purchase price.

If they are to be included in the sale, make sure these chattels are added to the purchase and sale agreement.

# Ranch and Farm Recreational Homes

Some people are looking to purchase a ranch or farm as a recreational home or hobby farm. This is a very specific enterprise and requires a certain level of experience. You need to consider what type of crops and/or animals can be raised on the land, what is required to maintain them, whether the property's borders are fenced, what facilities are included, and what the main residence is like. Figure out exactly what you have in mind and speak to a local agent who specializes in this type of property.

# Title and Ownership

When you are preparing to buy or sell a recreational property, you need to understand the different types of home ownership and the terminology used in land titles. The following are the most common types:

- Freehold
- Leasehold
- Strata title
- Co-operative
- Co-ownership (includes joint tenancy, tenancy in common, fractional and chapter ownership, timeshares)

## Freehold

A freehold interest is the same as ownership of property. The owner of a freehold interest has full use and control of the land and the buildings on it, subject to the rights of the Crown, local land-use bylaws, and any other restrictions in place at the time of purchase.

# Leasehold

A leasehold interest means that the building or structure such as a townhouse, apartment, or house is built on government-owned land. That is, only the building or structure and not the land can be bought and owned by individuals, and leasehold fees must be paid. The term leasehold can also apply to single-detached houses on farmland, on First Nations land, and so on.

Leasehold interests are for a defined period of time, and the term can either be fixed or ongoing. Frequently they are set for 99 years, in which case there will be no review of the lease rate for the full 99 years. After the term ends, the lease can usually be renewed. If the land lease does not have a fixed term, it will have periodic reviews of the lease rate, which is often done every 33 years.

The sale of a leasehold property differs greatly from the sale of a freehold property because the seller is only selling the improvements (the buildings) on the land, not the land itself. In the case of a 99-year lease, if the previous lessee had lived in a building on the leasehold land for 20 years, the new lessee would purchase the remaining portion of 79 years. The shorter the remaining portion, the less a buyer will pay for the leasehold.

Financing may be a big obstacle for buyers, as many institutions will not finance this type of sale. Ask your agent if he or she can provide a list of financial institutions that are receptive to financing leasehold interests.

# Strata title

In strata title, you not only own your unit, but you also share ownership of the common areas of the strata property, such as hallways, garages, and elevators. You share financial responsibility for their maintenance with the other owners of the building, and this is reflected in monthly maintenance fees.

# Co-operative

A co-operative is a type of ownership in which the property is owned in the name of a company or a registered association. Buyers purchase shares in the company, which gives them ownership of a suite (and often a parking stall as well).

In a condominium co-operative, you will be governed by the bylaws and regulations of the strata corporation or company. You will be required to follow these rules, and violations will result in fines. If you don't pay your monthly dues, assessments, and/or fines, the strata corporation or homeowners' association can put a lien on your home.

# Co-ownership

If you are purchasing a home with your spouse, family members, or friends, it is important to understand the different types of co-ownership. Co-ownership involves property owned by more than one person. This type of ownership is generally by joint tenancy or by tenancy in common. Your notary or lawyer should explain the differences between these two types of co-ownership in relation to your individual circumstances, and advise you about how you should be registered on the title.

## Joint tenancy

Joint tenancy is common among those purchasing with a spouse or partner. If you and your spouse purchase a property together as joint tenants, one partner becomes the sole owner when the other dies. The entire ownership automatically transfers to the survivor without having to go through probate. This feature is known as the right of survivorship. Thus, a joint tenant cannot leave the property in a will to a third party.

## Tenancy in common

Tenancy in common is a form of co-ownership among two or more owners, in which each owner may or may not have the same amount of shares or rights. One party may be able to sell his or her share without permission of the other parties. The following are examples of this form of co-ownership.

### Fractional ownership

Fractional ownership gives you a deeded share in a vacation residence and the right to use it for a specified amount of time per year, usually 4 to 12 weeks. With one-fifth ownership, for example, an owner co-owns the property with four others and is usually entitled to use the property for 10 weeks per year.

From a legal perspective, owning fractional real estate is relatively uncomplicated because each owner gets his or her own interest — that is, title and legal rights — to a fraction of the property. An owner is granted fee-simple ownership (i.e., absolute ownership with very few limitations), which is registered in the land title office. One owner can put a mortgage on the property or sell it or hand it down to children, independently of the other owners.

There are a number of different arrangements for fractional ownership, but often the property is located in a vacation resort, comes fully furnished, and has maintenance and upkeep handled by a property management company for an annual fee. All the owners contribute equally to the cost of management and maintenance, including regular and preventative repairs and a fund for the future replacement of furnishings. Some fractional real estate programs allow an owner to arrange a temporary exchange of property with an owner at another resort location.

Usage arrangements, ownership structures, and bylaws vary from property to property, so it is important to find out about each property and what particular arrangement would work for you. For example, be sure to investigate restrictions regarding vacation schedules and flexibility around "trading" time with another owner. A local agent can tell you what arrangements are available and how flexible these arrangements are. If you fail to get all the details before buying into a fractional property, this type of ownership may cause more problems than it is worth.

For many buyers, however, fractional real estate is their only option if they want to buy in an expensive market. With a budget of $300,000, for example, buyers could own a quarter ownership of a three-bedroom luxury townhouse in Whistler, one of Canada's top ski resorts, which would be worth more than $1.2 million for full ownership. Price and the ability to share the potential appreciation in value are among the advantages of fractional ownership.

Though fractional ownership can be very attractive, there is a downside. Financing fractional ownership is often challenging, as some lenders may not be familiar with this type of ownership. If you purchase fractional real estate that already has a lender, you may be in luck. If you can pay for it in cash, you may not have a problem at all.

### Chapters

A unique type of co-ownership that has recently surfaced is chapter ownership, in which a property is divided among ten owners — that is, a chapter owner shares ownership with nine others. Presently chapter ownership is unique to British Columbia, in places such as Whistler, and to some parts of the United States, such as Lake Tahoe in California and Aspen/Snowmass in Colorado. Owners are allotted five weeks per year — two weeks in the summer, two weeks in the winter, and one week whenever it is available.

Demographics for this type of ownership vary, and include both baby boomers and younger couples with children who are not able to afford a single-detached recreational home in vacation hot spots, which can have an average price of $1 million.

Baby boomers tend to enjoy the benefits of worry-free maintenance. However, such benefits usually come with a monthly price tag in the form of maintenance charges that can be quite costly. Make sure that if you purchase a chapter ownership, you take into account these additional monthly charges.

In any type of co-ownership, especially fractional ownership, find out your rights and obligations before you purchase. You will want to make sure you agree with all of the terms and conditions that are set out in the contract by either the previous owners or the project developers. In addition, it is advisable to consult your local agent to find out the legalities regarding ownership and resale of co-owned properties.

### Timeshares

A timeshare is a property that is owned by several people who each have a right to use it for certain periods each year. There are two categories of timeshare ownership: fee-ownership interest and right-to-use ownership.

In fee-ownership interest, the owner has absolute ownership for his or her share of the property, meaning he or she has a right to encumber, convey, or transfer the property for all future time.

In right-to-use ownership, the buyer receives no registrable title. This means you are not purchasing the property with full rights (as you would have with fee ownership). You only have the right to enjoy use of the property for specific periods of time.

Many provinces currently do not have legislation specifically addressing timeshare ownership. If you are considering buying or selling a timeshare, seek the advice of a lawyer or a real estate agent.

Recreational Property for Sale!

For Sale by Owner!

# Chapter 3
# ASSEMBLING YOUR TEAM OF PROFESSIONALS

Deciding on a real estate agent is your first step when forming your team of specialists that will assist you in your purchase of a recreational home. Your team of professionals should ensure that your legal interests are protected when you purchase your property. Take the time to assemble a local agent, a certified cottage or recreational-home inspector, and a lawyer or notary public who specializes in real estate.

## Real Estate Agent

Buying recreational real estate can be a very rewarding experience. Recreational-property owners generally feel a sense of pride in their property, and in the long term, they often gain financially. But the process of buying recreational real estate can be complex, and for this reason many buyers seek the help and professional expertise of a licensed agent who specializes in a specific type of property or geographic area.

The real estate industry is based on referrals, and agents receive their business from referrals from past clients, other agents, bankers, friends, or family members. Real estate agents also refer clients who are not within their specialized area to other agents.

## Responsibilities of your agent

Your agent can help you search for the right recreational home by determining with you what your needs and desires are. He or she can also help you assess your financial capability, list your expenditures and term payments, and calculate an appropriate down payment and monthly mortgage payment. Your financing will be finalized with a bank or other lending institution, but an agent can help you establish the price range you can afford to buy in.

Your agent can access the Multiple Listing Service (MLS), a computerized database of homes for sale. The MLS includes detailed information such as room-by-room measurements, property condition, agent's remarks, recent renovations, appliances, zoning, tax information, and other useful information to help you search for your ideal recreational home.

Your agent can also provide comparative data on similar properties and market statistics, and he or she can write legally binding offers. Agents can make your recreational-home buying experience easy and enjoyable and can save you a lot of time and money.

Your agent's duty is to provide clients with all the listed properties that meet the buyer's search criteria, including those with low commissions or no commissions. I strongly recommend that the relationship between the buyer and the real estate agent be in writing, in the form of a buyer-agent contract. This contract will ensure that both parties have a clear understanding of their rights and responsibilities, and know what to expect from each other.

Compensation to the real estate agent should be thoroughly discussed, including the amount of compensation, the sources of payment, and the time or occasion on which the payment is to be made.

### What is your relationship with a real estate agent?

As a recreational-home buyer, make sure that you understand your relationship with your agent. Be sure that the agent you choose to work with is always looking after your best interests.

A real estate agent must disclose to you any information obtained from any source that might influence your decision to purchase a recreational home. Also note that your agent cannot reveal to another person any confidential information you have disclosed to him or her that might jeopardize your bargaining position.

However, there are many instances in which an agent works with both the buyer and the seller. In this case, a dual agency is created, and the agent will negotiate for both parties. Both parties must feel comfortable with the agent, and they must agree to a dual agency in writing. It is important to understand that in this situation, as a buyer, any information you give to the agent must be passed on to the seller. As a safeguard against either the buyer or the seller feeling unfairly represented, it is always a good idea to retain your own buyer's agent to represent you.

## The exclusive buyer's agent contract

Some buyer's agents do not feel comfortable representing clients without having a contract signed by the buyer. This contract ensures that the prospective buyer is serious and won't take up the agent's time needlessly, as an agent only receives a commission when a sale is completed. Signing a buyer-agent agreement also ensures loyalty and that the agent is the only agent for the buyer.

An exclusive buyer-agent contract, when signed by both the buyer and the agent, is a legally binding contract. Read it carefully before signing to ensure that everything you are agreeing to is in writing. (See Sample 1.)

## Who pays the agent's commission?

Typically, the seller is responsible for the agent's commission, but the payment comes from the proceeds of the sale. If the property you are considering buying is a private sale, known as a For Sale by Owner (FSBO), in which case the buyer's agent is typically not compensated, you and your agent are advised to sign a commission agreement. In such cases, your agent will draw up a fee agreement between the buyer and the agent, specifying the fees and duties of each party. (See Sample 2.)

As a buyer, you have much to gain from an agent's services. If, after using the services and time of an agent, you decide not to buy, you are

## Sample 1
# BUYER–AGENT FEE AGREEMENT

### Agreement for Buyer to Pay a Commission

TO:_____
*(Real Estate Agent)*

In consideration of your endeavoring to effect a purchase of the property known as

_____,

and more particularly described as _____

_____, I hereby agree as follows:

Upon entering into a non-conditional Contract of Sale and Purchase with _____

_____ as Seller, I agree to pay

_____ a commission of
*(Real Estate Agent)*

_____ of the selling price.

The commission plus the applicable Goods and Services Tax will be paid upon completion of the sale.

Signed, Sealed, and Delivered this _____ day of _____ A.D. 20 _____

_____          _____
Witness                                                              Buyer

_____          _____
Print name                                                        Print name

_____          _____
Witness                                                              Buyer

_____          _____
Print name                                                        Print name

Accepted by _____
                              *(Real Estate Agent)*

                    _____
                                     *(Print name)*

          Per: _____

# Sample 2
# COMMISSION AGREEMENT

**COMMISSION AGREEMENT**         Date: _____

RE: _____

Further to the Listing Agreement dated _____, made

between _____ as Buyer and

_____ as Listing Agent and further to the
(Real Estate Agent)

Contract of Purchase and Sale dated _____

between _____ (Seller/s) and

_____ (Buyer/s), both of which

agreements cover the above referenced property, the undersigned hereby agree the commission payable

on the above noted transaction has been adjusted to _____

plus Goods and Services Tax. All other terms and conditions of the listing agreement remain the same and

in full force and effect.

_____      _____
Witness                                            Buyer

_____      _____
Print name                                    Print name

_____      _____
Witness                                            Buyer

_____      _____
Print name                                    Print name

Accepted by _____
(Real Estate Agent)

_____
(Print name)

Per: _____

not responsible for paying the agent, even if the agent spent a great deal of time with you looking for a recreational home. In fairness to agents, before you spend much of an agent's time, you should determine that you are in a financial position to purchase a property.

## What do agents do to earn their commission?

Some people think agents' commissions are disproportionately large compared with the amount of work they do. It is important to understand that the majority of work that agents do is behind the scenes. Agents spend a lot of time attending open houses, touring and viewing new properties that are for sale, and getting to know what is available on the market.

Agents also keep themselves current regarding changes in the market, property values, and interest rates. They also stay up to date on legal issues, tax breaks for their clients, and changes in building technology. The behind-the-scenes work that your agent does not only makes your search for the right recreational property easier, it also makes the process of buying the property more efficient.

## Are agents allowed to receive bonuses or other gifts from financial institutions?

To market their projects and properties, developers and property owners/sellers often provide agents with incentives such as bonuses on top of their commissions. Some financial institutions and mortgage brokers also provide agents who refer clients to their company with incentives such as bonuses, prizes, trips, or points in a points system. Such incentives are not uncommon in the real estate industry. They are acceptable as long as the agent informs the client about the incentive, whatever it may be.

## How do you choose an agent when buying a recreational property?

It is important that you choose an agent who specializes in the type of property you are looking for, whether that is a recreational property, a hobby farm, or other rural property. Most agents in this sector of the market specialize in a mix of rural residential, recreational property, and agricultural sales.

Choosing the right agent is paramount because many issues can come up when buying these types of properties — issues that are not commonplace with property sales in urban areas. For example, most cottage properties are only accessible by private easements, and there are potential problems arising from such access. An agent experienced with such situations would know how to handle this problem.

Other issues that you and your agent may encounter include regulations regarding the installation of wells and septic systems, and permit requirements for construction of waterfront improvements such as docks, wharfs, boathouses, and shoreline alterations. (See Chapter 6 for more information on these topics.) There are also environmental issues and statutes that impact on ownership and use of recreational properties.

## Do agents provide referrals to other professionals?

Frequently, buyers and sellers of homes ask agents to recommend other professionals, such as lawyers, notaries, mortgage brokers, and recreational-home inspectors. However, making specific recommendations may put agents at risk for liability if something goes wrong (e.g., if the buyer or seller is harmed in some way or if the cost of the service is higher than anticipated). The best solution is to ask your agent for a list of professionals with whom he or she has dealt in the past. Then you can call, interview, and choose your team of experts at your own convenience.

# The Difference between a Lawyer and a Notary Public

The roles and duties of lawyers and notaries public differ in each province. In some provinces, such as British Columbia and Quebec, notaries are not necessarily lawyers, but they can perform conveyancing duties (i.e., duties pertaining to the purchase and sale of real estate). In those provinces, retaining a notary public for conveyancing may be preferable because their fees are typically lower than lawyers' fees, and you can probably find a notary public in your neighbourhood.

One of the primary advantages of retaining a lawyer is that lawyers usually have a broad-based knowledge of the law and can provide legal assistance on issues that may be outside the scope of a notary public. For example, if it were necessary for a buyer to initiate legal action, the services of a lawyer or a notary with a law degree would be needed.

## Choosing a lawyer or notary public

Choosing your lawyer or notary public is a very important decision because this person will assist you from the time you have a binding contract to the day your property is legally yours, and perhaps even in the future. Professionalism, service, and trust are essential qualities to look for.

There are many ways to choose a lawyer or notary public. You can consult a lawyer or notary referral service in your community or call a lawyer/notary association for the names of lawyers who specialize in real estate. You can also ask friends, family, or colleagues for recommendations. Note that most lending institutions have a preferred list of lawyers and notaries they prefer to do business with, so check with your lender before hiring a lawyer or notary public.

Lawyers' and notaries' fees range widely, and the cost will also depend on the complexity of the transaction. When buying recreational real estate, the fees will likely be a minimum of $500 plus disbursements.

## The role of the lawyer or notary public

Retaining a lawyer or notary public ensures that your legal interests are protected when you buy your recreational home or property. The lawyer or notary gathers all the information needed to prepare the documents to transfer the property from the previous owner to the new owner. Here are some of the duties that lawyers and notaries may perform for you when you purchase your property:

- Receive and review the contract of purchase and sale
- Obtain confirmation of the buyer's and seller's full name and residency status
- Obtain the title search and common property search
- Confirm insurance coverage according to the lender's instructions
- Obtain copies of real estate encumbrances or subdivision plans from the land title office and obtain strata plans/special resolutions and review them with clients
- Confirm the payment of property taxes and arrange to pay outstanding taxes if necessary
- Confirm the payment of maintenance fees to a strata corporation
- Obtain a land survey
- Draft conveyance, mortgage, and support documentation
- Conduct a preregistration index search at the land title office and file documents for registration
- Conduct a post-registration index search after receiving registration numbers
- Receive and disburse trust funds

- Report to the strata management company regarding the sale of the unit
- Report to the agent and the municipality regarding the transfer of title

# Recreational-Home Inspectors

The home inspection industry in Canada is largely unregulated, so it is especially important that you research and hire a qualified home inspector. Talk to friends, family members, or neighbours in the area where you are buying who have recently hired an inspector and find out if they were happy with the inspector's work. Before hiring an inspector, you may want to look at the home inspectors' Standards of Practice and Code of Ethics, which can be found on the website of the Canadian Association of Home and Property Inspectors (CAHPI) at www.cahi.ca. These guidelines will give you an understanding of what a home inspector's responsibilities are. The CAHPI website also provides links to provincial branches of the association where you can research home inspectors in your area.

When writing your offer to purchase, make sure that the contract includes a clause about home inspection. The results of a proper inspection can be used to ask the seller to either fix problem areas or lower the selling price of the home to cover the cost of the necessary repairs. You may find that some sellers will adjust their price and others won't; with a thorough home inspector's report you will be in a better position to decide whether to proceed with the purchase or not.

A home inspection should include a complete assessment of the interior and exterior of the home, from roof to foundation, as well as an analysis of heating, plumbing, and electrical systems. Note that some areas of the home may not be easily accessible, such as crawl spaces that may be too small or too dangerous for inspectors to enter.

In addition to your home inspection, you should obtain a written evaluation of the property. A complete report should address in lay person's terms what was observed at that particular point in time, as well as problems that were uncovered.

Even if you are buying a new recreational home, you should hire an inspector to make sure that nothing was overlooked during the installation of such things as the electrical or plumbing systems. Also ensure that your certified cottage inspector has the necessary Errors and Omissions Insurance, which provides insurance coverage for lawsuits that are a result of the rendering of professional services.

Inspectors are generalists and may not be experts in any one field, such as air conditioning systems, heating systems, swimming pools, or furnaces. If you have a concern about a particular feature of the home, you may want to also hire an expert in that field to give his or her professional opinion.

# Environmental Experts

If you have retained the services of an agent specializing in recreational properties, he or she likely has a basic understanding of what environmental issues could arise. However, agents are not necessarily experts in matters of the environment. If the property condition disclosure statement, which provides a history and description of the condition of the property, including details of environmental, structural, and mechanical issues, mentions any environmental concerns, seek expert advice from a qualified professional. Make sure that you get advice about any environmental legislation that could affect your land or the water around or near your property.

# Protecting Your Legal Interest

As a buyer you can protect your legal interests by retaining qualified professionals who specialize in the purchase of properties — a real estate agent, a lawyer or notary public, a building inspector — all of whom can help you prepare the documentation and contract you need to purchase your recreational property. You can perform your own due diligence by reviewing disclosure statements, building inspection reports, title searches, Form "B", and building envelope reports.

Professionals such as lawyers, notaries public, appraisers, building inspectors, and agents are governed by industry-specific codes of ethics and standards of business practice. For example, the real estate industry is mandated by an organization called the Canadian Real Estate Association (CREA). CREA is one of Canada's largest single-industry trade associations, representing approximately 82,000 real estate brokers/agents and salespeople. CREA acts as a watchdog on national legislation that pertains to the real estate industry. CREA has frequently taken strong stands to defend the public's right to own and enjoy property.

The professionals you retain have a fiduciary duty to protect your legal interest, and they all carry Errors and Omissions Insurance. There are laws in place to protect you, the buyer, from a seller's misrepresentation or non-disclosure of hidden defects that could negatively affect your reasonable use and enjoyment of the property or its value. If you discover any latent defects or think the property was possibly misrepresented, seek legal advice as soon as possible.

## Title insurance

Title insurance can protect your legal interests in the event of human error due to improper documentation, and in cases of fraud or forgery. It insures against losses resulting from the following defects:

- Title and survey defects that would have been revealed by an up-to-date survey or real property report
- Fraud and forgery (e.g., forged documents and impersonations)
- Unmarketability of title (i.e., you are unable to sell your property until defects are fixed)
- Errors or omissions in the public registry
- Unregistered easements (e.g., utility, pipeline, etc.)
- Priority of other liens or encumbrances (mortgage or builder's liens)
- Executions or court judgments
- Undisclosed or missing heirs
- Errors in existing surveys, real property reports, or building location certificates
- Encroachment(s) on a neighbouring property (e.g., a fence or garage that you are ordered to remove because it is encroaching on a neighbour's property)
- Zoning setback violations or easements (rights-of-way)
- No legal access to the property (no right-of-way)
- Municipal zoning and bylaw infractions
- Violations of subdivision, development, or other agreements

You can get title insurance through your lawyer or notary public upon closing, when all the obligations in a contract of purchase and sale have been met.

## C h a p t e r   4
# FINANCING

Although it is sometimes confusing and intimidating, with the assistance of a local agent and mortgage broker, financing a recreational property can be easier than you think.

## How Do You Get Financing for a Recreational Property?

Financing for real estate can be obtained from your bank or credit union. However, some banks or trust companies will not finance certain properties, such as land for recreation and/or development, or land that is vacant. In this case, you may want to speak to mortgage companies that specialize in these types of properties. Your agent can probably suggest which lenders to approach in your area. Another option for some buyers is that some owners of recreational properties offer financing for their properties.

## What Are the Types of Mortgage Loans?

When you are considering buying recreational property, it's important to become familiar with some of the terms commonly used when referring to mortgages.

### Conventional mortgage

This type of mortgage loan requires a down payment of at least 25 percent of the purchase price or of the appraised value of the recreational property, whichever is less. This type of mortgage may translate into savings for the borrower because the borrower does not have to pay a mortgage insurance premium. (Mortgage insurance is usually necessary to protect the lender if the payments are not made — see the section called Mortgage Insurance later in this chapter.)

## High-ratio mortgage

A high-ratio mortgage loan allows you to borrow more than 75 percent of the purchase price or the appraised value of the property, whichever is less. But you must pay a mortgage default insurance premium. This premium can be as much as 3.75 percent of the loan amount.

## Insured mortgage

An insured mortgage allows you to put as little as 5 percent of the property's value as the down payment and obtain a high-ratio mortgage that is equivalent to the remaining 95 percent. You must meet certain qualifications regarding your income and monthly debts.

## Assumable mortgage

Sometimes a vendor will already have a mortgage on the recreational home that you want to buy. Instead of going through the process of obtaining another mortgage, you can sometimes assume the existing mortgage from the vendor. This is called an assumable mortgage.

When you assume the vendor's mortgage, you continue making the monthly payments for the remaining term of the mortgage, at the same interest rate as the vendor had. You will need the lender's approval, and you will have to pass a credit check, just as you would if you applied for a new mortgage.

You may possibly assume a mortgage with a low interest rate even when the current interest rates are high, because the vendor obtained the mortgage several years earlier when interest rates were lower. By assuming the mortgage, you may also be helping the vendor. Because most lenders charge a penalty if a borrower repays a mortgage in full before its term expires, by passing the mortgage along to you instead of repaying the lender the entire sum, the vendor avoids this penalty. In some cases the vendor may lower the price of the home to reflect this saving.

## Condominium mortgage

In a condominium mortgage, the buyer of a condominium unit receives legal title to the unit he or she is purchasing as well as partial title to the common areas. This means that you can sell your unit and your share of the common areas without having to ask permission from others who own units in the building.

## Open mortgage

Some lenders will offer open mortgages for vacation homes. An open mortgage means that you can repay the loan, in part or in full, at any time without penalty. Interest rates are usually higher on this type of loan. An open mortgage can be a good choice if you plan to sell your recreational home in the near future. Most lenders will allow you to convert to a closed mortgage at any time. Many experts suggest taking an open mortgage for a short term in times of high rates and converting to a closed mortgage when rates fall.

## Closed mortgage

A closed mortgage usually offers the lowest interest rate available at any given time. It's a good choice if you'd like to have a fixed mortgage payment that you can budget for. However, closed mortgages are not flexible, and there are often penalties or restrictive conditions attached to prepayments or additional lump-sum payments. It may not be the best choice if you might sell your recreational home before the end of the term.

## Vendor take-back (VTB) mortgage

A vendor take-back (VTB) mortgage allows you a chance to purchase a property with the help of vendors who lend you a portion of the purchase price. Such a loan often comes with favourable or flexible terms, depending on the inclinations of the individual vendor. The loan may be open, which means that you can repay it at any time without penalty. The vendor may charge an interest rate lower than the prevailing market rate, or the vendor may negotiate the term of the loan with you.

You can avoid a lot of red tape and administrative charges by obtaining a VTB mortgage. In a slow market, a VTB mortgage attracts potential buyers. If the market is hot, you won't find many vendors who'll offer to lend you money at favourable rates, unless their property is poorly located, in bad condition, or otherwise hard to sell. In general, vendors sometimes prefer the steady and consistent return of a mortgage secured by a familiar property to a riskier investment. They also prefer borrowers such as you, whom they will get to know and trust, to faceless and nameless managers who manage many other types of investments.

## Portable mortgage

A portable mortgage means that the lender will arrange a mortgage loan that can be transferred to another property if you decide to move. Note that not all lenders offer portable mortgages.

Make sure that you have a portable mortgage on your principal residence, as this allows you to transfer your mortgage to another property. Note that there may be some restrictions from lenders on the value and type of property to which you will be transferring the mortgage.

## Reverse mortgage

If you own your principal residence outright and you are older than 62, you may opt to obtain a reverse mortgage. This is a variation on the traditional mortgage concept, and allows a homeowner to take out a "loan" against the home, and convert some of the equity (the accumulated net value of the home) into cash or a stream of income payments while still retaining ownership and possession of the home. In this way, you can borrow equity from your primary home to finance a recreational home. No repayment of the loan is necessary until a specified time in the future: when the homeowner sells, when the homeowner moves permanently, when a preset period ends (perhaps five or ten years), or when the homeowner dies.

Reverse mortgages also differ from the traditional mortgage in other ways. Since the homeowner receives payments or equity advances rather than making monthly payments, the balance owing on a reverse mortgage increases over time, while the homeowner's share of the equity in the home decreases. While semi-annual compounding is common in reverse mortgages, the frequency of compounding in these mortgages currently has no legal limit.

## Blanket mortgage

If you already have a mortgage on a property and take on another mortgage for your recreational property, you have a "blanket mortgage." That is, one mortgage that applies to two or more properties. In this situation, an appraisal of both of your properties is typically required. This may mean some out-of-pocket expenses for you as not all financial institutions will incur these charges.

A blanket mortgage eliminates the need for you to provide another down payment and, because of the appraisal process, takes care of any questions and concerns a financial institution might otherwise have about whether your recreational home has year-round access, an up-to-date survey, and a septic system, and whether the water supply needs testing. In the event of default, the lender could proceed against one or both of the properties in order to get sufficient proceeds from the sale to satisfy the outstanding debt.

## Vacation property mortgage

Your final option is to arrange for a vacation property mortgage. There are a few differences between a vacation property mortgage and a residential mortgage. Usually interest rates are 0.5 to 1 percent higher than residential mortgage rates, and you need a down payment of at least

25 percent — in fact, a 40 percent down payment is not uncommon. In addition, standards for septic systems, surveys, and water samples must be met.

# Mortgage Insurance

Whenever you take out a mortgage, you will be required to take out insurance on that mortgage. You should be aware of the different components of mortgage insurance.

## Mortgage default insurance

Mortgage default insurance ensures that the lender will not lose any money if you default on your mortgage (i.e., cannot make your mortgage payments) and if the value of your property is not sufficient to repay your mortgage debt. The insurer can either be the Canada Mortgage and Housing Corporation (CMHC) or a private insurance company. Because there is no risk of losing money, lenders have confidence to make mortgage loans of up to 95 percent of the purchase price of the home (subject to price ceilings). This means that your down payment can be as little as 5 percent of the price of the recreational home.

Mortgage default insurance has two components: an application fee and an insurance premium. The application fee typically ranges from $75 to $235, and is required by law by most Canadian lending institutions on all mortgage loans that exceed 75 percent of the appraised property value.

Insurance premiums range from 0.5 to 3.75 percent of the amount of your mortgage loan, depending on the size of the loan and the value of your home. The premium can be added to your mortgage loan and become part of your regular mortgage payments, or it can be paid off in a lump sum at the time of purchase to save interest charges on the premium itself.

## Mortgage Interest Rate

A major influence on your decision about when to buy is the mortgage interest rate. What rates are available now, and what will they be in the future? Will they fall or will they rise, and if they rise, by how much? Trying to answer these questions can be difficult, and CMHC's Market Analysis Centre can help. They can provide you with both an analysis of the current mortgage market and an outlook for future mortgage rates. For those who need the big picture of Canadian housing, the Market Analysis Centre produces a series of national and local reports that provide a comprehensive view of housing across the country. These are available on their website at www.cmhc-schl.gc.ca.

# Mortgages for Vacant Land

Financing issues must be addressed when purchasing vacant land — that is, land that does not have any buildings or structures. Under CMHC's guidelines, 50 percent of the total purchase price is required as a down payment. Many financial institutions will not finance this type of property, so inquire with your mortgage broker or credit union for more information.

# How Much Down Payment Do You Need?

When purchasing a cottage or recreational home, most buyers need some form of financing. Lending institutions will usually advance anywhere from 60 to 75 percent of the purchase price or the appraised value, whichever is the lesser amount. Some lenders will take into consideration whether your cottage or recreational home is a winterized, year-round home, has safe drinking water, and meets septic and survey requirements. Further, the cottage or recreational home must be more than 800 square feet and on a permanent foundation. If a property meets all of a lending institution's requirements, it may offer a mortgage of 95 percent of the appraised value or purchase price (whichever is less), subject to mortgage insurance.

# Appraisals

Banks require appraisals for recreational homes to determine the home's value. Note that adequate time is needed for an appraisal as the property may be difficult to access or in a remote area, or there may only be a handful of appraisers available. During periods of high sales activities, it may even be more difficult to get an appraiser on short notice.

# The Documents the Lender Will Require

Lenders want plenty of financial information about you (and your co-buyers, if applicable) to assess your ability to repay a loan. Checklist 1 will help you gather the necessary documents.

## Checklist 1
## GATHERING THE DOCUMENTS FOR THE LENDER

- ❏ Details of employment, including proof of income (T4 slips, personal income tax returns, a letter from your employer stating your position)
- ❏ Other sources of income (e.g., pension or rental income documents)
- ❏ Current banking statements
- ❏ Down payment verification
- ❏ Written consent for the lender to perform a credit check
- ❏ List of liabilities (e.g., credit card balances, car loans)
- ❏ Financial statement outlining total debts owed and monthly payments
- ❏ Copy of valid appraisal report (if recent) or proof of available funds for appraisal fees
- ❏ Copy of property listing
- ❏ Copy of the agreement of purchase and sale (if it's a resale home)
- ❏ Plans and cost estimates of a new recreational home
- ❏ Condominium financial statements, if applicable
- ❏ Certificate for the water supply and septic tank, if applicable

# Chapter 5
# OWNERSHIP AND TAXATION

Owners of vacation homes or secondary residences cannot ignore the matter of taxes. As will be discussed in Chapter 20, capital gains tax is payable on secondary homes, including cottages and timeshares. For the recreational-home buyer, this is not of immediate concern, but it should be kept in mind if you are buying property for investment purposes. Buyers need to know about GST/HST and property taxes, as these tax issues directly impact on the cost of your purchase.

## GST/HST

The Goods and Services Tax (GST) is a form of value-added tax, similar to the taxes levied in member countries of the European Union, and in New Zealand and Australia. The GST is 7 percent at the time of publication of this book; it may be subject to change. It applies to the purchase price of newly constructed and substantially renovated homes. Note that GST is not charged on older homes. Ask your real estate agent, notary, or lawyer for further information

as to whether the GST is included or excluded in the purchase price.

In 1997, the provinces of New Brunswick, Nova Scotia, and Newfoundland and Labrador repealed their existing retail sales taxes in order to harmonize them with the GST. The tax, commonly referred to as the Harmonized Sales Tax (HST), is 15 percent, which comprises a 7 percent federal tax and an 8 percent provincial tax.

**Note:** Provincial sales tax (PST) is not applied to real estate purchases.

## Property/Land Transfer Tax (British Columbia and Ontario)

When an application is made at a land title office to register changes to a certificate of title, a land registration tax must be paid. This is referred to as the Property Transfer Tax in BC, and the Land Transfer Tax in Ontario. This tax is not the same as yearly property taxes, which are for services that are received from the local government.

In British Columbia, the rate is 1 percent on the first $200,000 of the property's fair market value, and if the property value is over $200,000, an additional 2 percent of the amount that exceeds $200,000. For more information, visit the website of the Government of BC's Property Taxation Branch at www.rev.gov.bc.ca/rpt/.

In Ontario, the rate is 0.5 percent on the first $55,000 of the transfer value; plus 1 percent of the amount that exceeds $55,000 and is up to $250,000; plus 1.5 percent of the amount that exceeds $250,000 and is up to $400,000; plus 2 percent of the amount that exceeds $400,000. This calculation only applies to land that contains at least one and not more than two single-family dwellings.

# Property Classes

There are standard property classes for the purposes of assessment and taxation in each province. For example, in Ontario there are seven classes — residential/farm, multi-residential, commercial, industrial, pipeline, farmlands, and managed forests — but only two would apply to recreational properties:

- *Residential/Farm*: This includes single-family dwellings, seasonal dwellings/ recreational property, manufactured homes, some vacant land, and farm buildings that do not belong under the "farmlands" classification.

- *Multi-residential*: This includes multi-family residences such as duplexes, apartments, and condominiums, as well as seasonal dwellings/recreational property, manufactured homes, and some vacant land.

Additional property classes are identified from time to time by provincial governments. How your recreational property is classified will determine the rate of property taxes assessed.

# Property Tax Assessment

The amount of property taxes payable will affect how much money you can borrow to finance your purchase. Find out the annual property tax by asking the seller for a copy of the latest property assessment and/or contacting the municipality's property assessment office.

## Who pays for the property taxes of the current year?

If the current owner has already paid the full year's property taxes to the municipality, you will have to reimburse them for your share of the year's taxes. The tax year is from January 1 to December 31 of each year. However, the payment dates vary. For example, in Whistler, BC, taxes are payable in July of each year. In Barrie, Ontario, property taxes are due quarterly. The actual dates depend on which city ward the property is located. (Generally, the dates fall in the last week or so of February, April, July, and September.)

You will be required to pay your share of taxes from the adjustment date set out in the contract of purchase and sale. This adjustment will be made by your legal representative and will be included in the purchase price.

# Chapter 6
# LAND AND WATER ISSUES

There are many specialties within the real estate industry. Key differences between urban and rural real estate practice can potentially become dangerous liabilities if the agent you have chosen has little experience in rural real estate. Consider working with an agent who specializes in this, or better yet, who has worked in the locations you are interested in. It is up to the agent to have an understanding of the local area and ensure that the buyer and seller are informed of all pertinent concerns.

## Maps

Maps are a great way to determine whether or not a property is ideal for you. Before purchasing any recreational property, find out from your agent whether the seller has any maps of the property and its surroundings. If not, then your agent should help you find and interpret the necessary maps of the area. The following are some of the maps you may come across.

## Forest recreation map

You will find that a forest recreation map has the most recent information about roads, trails, geographical features, recreational sites, and campgrounds. Contact the local forestry office to acquire this type of map.

## Topographic map

Topographic maps are general purpose reference maps with full-colour features including contours, which show if an area is hilly, steep, or swampy. They include natural features such as valleys, lakes, rivers, and wooded areas, as well as man-made features such as buildings, powerlines, roads, dams, cut lines, access trails, and park boundaries. Canadian topographic maps are published by the federal government in both paper and digital formats. You can order them online at http://maps.nrcan.gc.ca.

## Plan

A plan is a large-scale and detailed map of a small area, such as the lot of a property. You can determine the size and measurement of the lot and where the roads are located. To obtain this map, ask the local agent, land registry office, or title agency office.

## Agricultural land reserve map (BC)

Many provinces have land-use policies designed to protect and preserve agricultural land. For example, in 2002 British Columbia created the Agricultural Land Commission Act. If you are buying rural property in BC, consult an agricultural land reserve map to determine if your property is on an agricultural land reserve. At the same time, check with the Land Commission whether the property is affected by the rules in the act; their records take precedence over certificates of title. In addition, examine the community plans and/or local bylaws to determine the effect, if any, the Agricultural Land Commission Act has on the property.

## Surveys and Survey Certificates

Although the listing agent is responsible for the accuracy of the property information listing, including lot size, floor areas of buildings, and zoning, it is the buyer's responsibility to verify that the information is correct, especially when dealing with recreational properties, because lot boundaries that are given may not always be accurate.

A survey certificate defines the boundaries of the property and indicates where the home stands on the property. Typically it is handed down from one owner to the next, so be sure to ask the seller for it. However, if any additions, extensions, or improvements have been made to the home or land since the previous survey, you may want to get a new survey done.

## Hiring a surveyor

When selecting a surveyor, consider hiring the surveyor who did the most recent survey of the property because he or she would have survey notes and previous experience with the property, which could save you some money. The owners may be able to tell you who the previous surveyor was or the surveyor's name may be written on the survey certificate.

Surveyors vary in price and are regulated by the municipality. They may charge for the distance travelled as well as an hourly fee. Ask the local agent for a list of local land surveyors with whom he or she has worked in the past.

## Survey notes

Survey notes are notes that were taken by the surveyor when he or she was setting up the original corner posts to the property. The surveyor's notes describe distinguishing features of the property, such as specific trees or significant landmarks. These notes can be requested from the Surveyor General's office. If the corner posts are not visible, the notes will help you find where the original corner posts were so you can re-walk the property lines if necessary.

## Geotechnical survey

A geotechnical survey is a survey using a variety of tests that check the stability of the property's soil, rock, and slope. This ensures a safe foundation when buildings are erected on the property. These tests are done using a variety of methods, including using radar.

## Land Issues
### Land title search

A land title search will let you know who is registered as the current owner of the property and if there are any registered mortgages, easements, rights-of-way, or restrictive covenants that may affect the use or value of the property. This information should also be provided by the seller in a property condition disclosure statement or in the agreement of purchase and sale, but do not rely on those documents for full disclosure. If you are not sure about what the title search is telling you, ask a qualified person, such as a lawyer or agent, to explain its terms.

### Right-of-way and easement

The terms "right-of-way" and "easement" are often used interchangeably, but their meanings differ somewhat. "Statutory right-of-way" refers to the legal right given to a governmental or quasi-governmental body to use a portion of a private property (for example, to install a pipeline or construct a road).

An "easement" is the right given to others to pass over or make limited use of another person's land, commonly for access. Rights-of-way and easements are common with recreational properties — for example, a lakefront house with a public walkway to the lake, or a property that can only be accessed by a private road that is located on another person's property.

An easement can be for a limited period, such as until completion of a subdivision, or it may be granted forever. In the latter instance, once the easement is granted, it will pass from one owner to the next. An easement is not restricted to an adjacent property.

It is important to get all documentation about rights-of-way and easements in writing whenever possible so that the buyer and the buyer's representatives, such as a lawyer or an agent, can also read this documentation.

### Restrictive covenants

A restrictive covenant is a legal obligation imposed on a deed by the seller that requires the buyer to do or refrain from doing certain things on the property. The intent is to protect neighbouring properties from harm to property values. Restrictive covenants can be found, for example, in subdivisions where all the owners are obliged to conform to various stipulations. These covenants can regulate such matters as the height and location of fences and can prohibit satellite dishes, clothes lines, storing of motorhomes (unless in enclosed areas), and planting certain trees, shrubs, or other vegetation.

## Setback

A setback refers to a distance from the lot boundary in which no structures may be built in accordance with zoning bylaws. Setbacks are normally detailed for front, side, or rear yards in relation to main and accessory structures.

In addition to land setbacks, there may be setback requirements or other restrictions on cliffs and on property that is adjacent to streams, rivers, oceans, or lakes. Such setbacks on property adjacent to water are intended to preserve the water or upland habitat.

## Access roads

Rights-of-way for passage or road widening should be surveyed and registered; if this applies to your property, ask your real estate agent or lawyer to confirm if the modifications were registered. Note that driveways and culverts may not be constructed on any public roads without the permission of your province's ministry of transportation or highways.

## Buying acreage or vacant land

I cannot stress enough how important it is to get as much information about the property before purchasing vacant land. If you are thinking about purchasing vacant land, acquiring a permit to build on it may become difficult. For example, if a property in Ontario is part of land that is environmentally protected, the Ministry of Natural Resources will not grant building permits. Unfortunately, for real estate buyers in Ontario, whether they are buying vacant land or even land already containing some buildings, there is no public registry to find out if construction on the property has been frozen by the Environmental Protection Act.

Make sure a property condition disclosure statement is provided by the seller, as it should alert you to any such issues.

## Profit à prendre

Profit à prendre is a written agreement which gives the holder the right to enter and take something from a property, such as soil, petroleum, timber, and minerals on the premises. The right can, in some instances, pass with title upon the sale of the property.

## Mineral rights

The owner of land may or may not have title to the minerals (coal, oil, gas, etc.) on or in the land. There may be separate titles for ownership of minerals and ownership of surface (land) rights, which means that owning the land does not mean automatically owning the mineral rights. The rights of ownership to mines and minerals can be transferred in much the same manner as land is sold and transferred. If the land you are considering has mines or minerals on it, get legal advice. It is possible that the titles through which mineral rights are bought and sold are reserved by the Crown.

## First Nations lands

If you are considering buying or leasing First Nations land, seek legal and expert advice as soon as possible. Your agent should be aware that dealing with First Nations reserve lands requires special knowledge. Fundamentally, the Indian Act states that reserve lands are held by the Crown for the use and benefit of First Nations. To convey such property to other persons, the land must first of all be surrendered to

the federal government. The government in turn may convey titles by way of sale, or grant leases on the surrendered land.

# Water Issues
## Waste management systems

Most houses in developed areas are connected to a municipal sewer system that allows waste from a house to drain into sewer pipes. The waste is carried to a treatment facility before being released into the environment.

In less developed areas, waste disposal is not centrally managed; the disposal systems are often located on an individual's property and are governed by provincial environmental regulations. This means installing and maintaining a septic system on your property. Many older cottages have crude septic systems. If additions are made to the living space of the cottage, these systems may no longer be adequate: a new septic system may be required (at considerable cost).

Recreational property owners must comply with the provisions of the federal Environmental Protection Act. Infractions can result in fines and possibly being required to remove the existing waste disposal system from the premises. For this reason, buyers should educate themselves about the current septic system. If the seller doesn't know much about it, ask the seller's agent for more information. Look at the property condition disclosure statement or contact the municipal office for more information.

### Sewage disposal inspections

If you are purchasing a property with an on-site sewage disposal system, make sure that your home inspector is qualified to inspect this system. In Ontario, for example, sewage system inspectors must be approved under the qualifications established by the Ontario Building Code. The code applies not only to sewage system inspectors but also to persons engaged in the construction, repair, maintenance, and cleaning or emptying of sewage systems. Find out from your agent whether the sewage system was installed with the approval and the inspection of the appropriate department of the provincial government.

In the case of a property without an on-site sewage disposal system, your contract of purchase and sale should provide a clause allowing you, the buyer, to obtain approval for an application for a disposal permit. Be aware that applying for a permit does not guarantee that it will be granted. In British Columbia, for example, the government's process for a sewage disposal permit allows for a 30-day waiting period following the approval during which any person with a legitimate reason may protest the issuance. Buyers who proceed to install a system without waiting 30 days may be required to alter or remove the system.

## Chemical, environmentally friendly, and composting toilets

If you are looking to buy recreational property in an area where there is a shortage of water, consider the option of using chemical, environmentally friendly, or composting toilets.

Chemical toilets are toilets consisting of a seat or bowl attached to a container holding a chemical solution that changes waste into sludge. These toilets are found on airplanes, trains, and buses as well as in recreational homes where indoor plumbing is not available. You can identify these toilets by the blue-coloured dye in the bowl.

A new variation on chemical toilets is the environmentally friendly toilet. The same size and shape as a regular toilet, it uses degradable waste bags that gel waste, neutralize odour, and begin the decay process. This system is promoted as being spill proof and hygienic, as well as economical and waterless. It can be used in a cabin, boat, or RV.

Composting toilets are also environmentally friendly, as they use no water, are odour free, create no pollution, and work with nature to produce fertilizer and evaporate liquids. They come in a variety of styles and sizes, and are particularly suitable for properties without septic tanks.

### Grey water

Grey water is water that has been used in a home for washing dishes, bathing, or doing laundry and that is suitable for reuse. Reusing grey water serves two purposes: it reduces the amount of fresh water needed to supply a household and the amount of waste water entering sewer or septic systems. Find out whether the recreational property you are considering buying has a system for reusing grey water. This is especially important in locations where there may be a shortage of water.

## Water supply

In the case of an unproven water supply from either an existing or a new source, the buyer should be concerned not only with the quality, but the quantity. Ask the seller detailed questions about the water supply, read the property condition disclosure statement carefully, and provide a clause in the contract of purchase and sale whenever water supply may be an issue.

### Water and contamination testing

If a supply of drinking water comes from a well or other non-municipal source, then the quality and safety of that water are important considerations for the buyer. Every owner should be aware of the quality of water and test it on a regular basis. Ask to see test results, or bring in a professional to do the testing.

There are two ways to test water — through chemical analysis and microbiological analysis. A general microbiological analysis can verify if there is coliform or fecal streptococcus in the water. Testing requirements can differ depending on the provincial or territorial jurisdiction. For more information, read the applicable Water Resources Act or Water Protection Act, or contact the Ministry of Environment in your province or territory. In general, most water problems can be solved using treatment systems specifically designed to remove contaminants.

### Water wells

Water wells, whether they are drilled, bored, or dug, are all subject to legislative control. The Ministry of the Environment is responsible for the protection of water quantity and quality.

Buyers should ask the sellers about seasonal variation in the water supply. An experienced well user may say that the water supply has been adequate for his or her needs, but may not realize that a buyer from the city often requires more water. It is not unusual for shallow wells to dry up during extended periods of low rainfall. In some cases, this may require having water delivered to the property during these periods.

In other locations, flooding may be more of a concern: you may want to ask what the water table is like throughout the year, especially if you are thinking of constructing a basement.

Some water quality problems can be easily detectable by taste, colour, or odour. If a buyer is concerned about water quality, he or she should contact the local health district, the provincial Ministry of Health, or Health Canada.

### Cisterns or water holding tanks

A cistern is a rainwater catchment system composed of a water-collection system, a storage holding tank, and a water distribution system. Rainwater harvesting systems can reduce the use of municipal water and provide additional water in areas where well water is depleted during dry periods.

### Heated waterlines

In some recreational areas, properties may have heated waterlines that are specially designed for a year-round water supply. This typically consists of an automatic thermostatic control combined with a heating element that extends through a plastic waterline. In temporary situations, these lines may lie on the ground. The heating elements can also be installed in existing waterlines. In locations with cold winters, find out from your realtor and a certified recreational-home inspector whether this feature exists on the property you are considering buying.

## Flood plains

If you are purchasing a home, make sure that the property is not on a flood plain or other area designated as having a higher than average risk of natural disasters such as flooding or mud slides. In some provinces, you can view floodplain maps at regional water management offices. Check the property condition disclosure statement from the seller for any mention of susceptibility to flooding. Verify with the insurance provider what is and is not covered in a homeowner policy.

## Marine (submerged) cables

In certain areas telephone and hydro cables extend underwater to service locations. These marine cables have typically been used to provide services where land and above-water connections would be too expensive or not feasible. For example, some islands off the coast of British Columbia have marine cables for utilities.

Provincial environmental requirements have curtailed the use of these cables, and in some cases, new installations have been refused. Permits may encounter delays, and applications may not be granted final approval. If submerged cables provide utilities to your property, contact the applicable department and/or ministry responsible for environmental legislation.

# Shorelines properties

Waterfront cottages are subject to numerous regulatory bodies, both federal and provincial, which control what can and cannot be done with beaches and shorelines and the beds of most lakes, rivers, and streams to the high-water mark. Permits are required for alterations to shorelines, dredging, construction of docks, boathouses, and other water-related projects. Regulatory authorities are empowered to enforce federal and provincial legislation. They may, for example, prevent cottage owners from making additions to existing buildings, installing new structures in sensitive areas of a property, altering the slope of the land in any way, or placing fill in certain areas. To safeguard and preserve the natural flora and fauna, some provincial authorities have been reluctant to approve projects that would alter the shoreline or waterbed in any way.

Information about shorelines should be included in any agreement of purchase and sale to warrant the legality of any current structures and to ensure intended changes can be made in the near future.

## Riparian rights

A riparian right is the right of an owner to use and enjoy the water that flows across or along his or her land. It includes the right of the owner to make use of the water area for boathouses, fishing, and so on. Riparian rights are frequently subject to provincial legislation concerning public lands and other environmental legislation that affects shoreline property.

## Shoreline ownership

In Ontario, the Strategic Lands Initiative, which was initiated by the Ministry of Natural Resources (MNR), can affect the owners of shoreline property. Many property owners have inadvertently encroached on Crown land when they improved cottages and lakefront homes. The MNR is currently in the process of obtaining new surveys for many of these shorelines, and if owners have encroached on Crown land, they are approached to either purchase or lease the Crown land that was affected.

In Prince Edward Island, the Regulatory and Appeals Commission is an independent tribunal that administers land ownership legislation and hears appeals on issues relating to land use. For example, a corporation cannot have an aggregate landholding in excess of five acres or have a shore frontage in excess of 165 feet unless it first receives permission from the Lieutenant Governor in Council.

## Docks

If you are planning to build a dock, it is important to know that the construction of docks normally requires municipal approval as well as approval from the appropriate provincial or territorial ministry and/or department. Permits are usually granted with various conditions, most of which are designed to protect the environment. Some conditions are as follows:

- In-water work to be completed between Labour Day and March of the following year
- Turbidity to be kept to a minimum
- Dredged materials to be stabilized to prevent erosion
- Wood treatment chemicals such as creosote preservative not to be used

In addition, building permits are required from municipal authorities.

## Waterways

Conservation authorities are also responsible for reviewing and issuing permits for any alteration to waterways. As a general guideline, conservation authorities promote natural design as opposed to straightening of watercourses, as straightening would compromise natural fish habitats.

## Dredging

When dredging in or near watercourses, you may require a permit from municipal, regional, and/or provincial departments. Contact the provincial or territorial ministry of the environment or natural resources for detailed information, current regulations, and permit applications. Note that dredging of waterways in federal parks or along federal canals requires approval from Parks Canada. The intent of these guidelines is to help conserve fish habitat and natural areas surrounding these watercourses.

## Building a bridge or culvert

Should you wish to construct a bridge that spans over a river or road, or a culvert that involves some type of drainage or a channel under a road or sidewalk, regulatory approval may be needed from several levels of government. In Ontario, you should contact the Ministry of Natural Resources for guidance on whether a work permit is required, if other municipal or related approvals are needed, and what are the specific environmentally appropriate practices and procedures. Local conservation authorities are also involved in the approval process. For properties fronting the Rideau Canal or Trent-Severn Waterway, the owner should also contact Parks Canada. Large culverts may even require Canadian Coast Guard approval under the Navigable Waters Protection Act.

If you want to build a wooden structure near water, good choices of wood are cedar or hemlock. Both have natural preservatives that protect them from rotting, which results from repeated exposure to water and air-drying. Less expensive types of wood can be used for underwater construction, where the wood will not be exposed to the air.

## Reused and recycled materials

Although it is generally in the best interest of the environment to reduce, reuse, and recycle, there are circumstances where using recycled materials is problematic. Reused materials such as oil drums, tires, or car parts are not recommended for shoreline or in-water work as these materials often release oils, grease, and other chemical substances that are toxic to humans, fish, and other forms of wildlife.

## Wetlands

Wetlands are areas that are covered by shallow water or where the water table is at or near the surface. There are five types of wetlands — swamps, bogs, fens, marshes, and open water less than two metres in depth. One of the goals of conservation authorities is to protect and conserve wetland areas whenever possible. In Ontario, for example, the Ministry of Natural Resources has identified Areas of Natural and Scientific Interest (ANSIs) to help protect representative and special natural areas, plants, and animals. In wetlands that are classified as ANSI, prior to new developments being approved, environmental impact studies are required and appropriate action is taken to ensure that the wetland function is maintained or enhanced.

## Legislation and regulatory bodies

It is beyond the scope of this book to address the various federal, provincial/territorial, and regional regulatory bodies that have jurisdiction over water issues. You should be aware, however, that there may be regulations relating to conservation and the environment in the area where you are buying recreational property. The federal Fisheries Act applies across Canada; the Niagara Escarpment Commission and the Islands Trust Fund are examples of two regional bodies that may affect recreational land in Ontario and British Columbia respectively.

## Fisheries Act

The federal Fisheries Act provides for the protection of fish habitat. Under this act, no one may carry out any work that harmfully alters, disrupts, or destroys fish habitat, unless formal authorization is given by Fisheries and Oceans Canada.

The act also states that no one is permitted to deposit a harmful substance into water that would contaminate fish. Violations can result in substantial fines, even imprisonment, and a requirement to cover the costs of returning the site to its original state.

## Niagara Escarpment Commission

The Niagara Escarpment is an environmentally significant area stretching from Niagara Falls northward to Bruce Peninsula. The Niagara Escarpment Commission, established under the Niagara Escarpment Planning and Development Act, is responsible for and ensuring that only such development occurs as is compatible with the natural environment of the Niagara Escarpment.

## Islands Trust Fund

Between the British Columbia mainland and Vancouver Island there are countless small islands and thirteen main islands — the Northern and Southern Gulf Islands — which are part of the Islands Trust Fund, whose vision is "to create a legacy of special places, protecting both natural and cultural features in perpetuity, in order to help sustain the unique character and environment of the Islands Trust Area." The Islands Trust Fund currently has 60 protected areas established and carefully managed for conservation. If you are thinking of buying property in the Gulf Islands, be sure to check whether it comes under the jurisdiction of the Islands Trust Fund.

# Chapter 7
# BUYER BEWARE!

This chapter looks at a range of issues that you should be aware of if you are considering buying a recreational home. Not all of these problems will be of concern in all regions of the country, but knowing about them can save you from making a purchase that could bring you heartache (and possible financial ruin) instead of relaxation and enjoyment.

## Protect Yourself from a "Leaky Condo"

"Leaky condo syndrome" is defined as catastrophic failure of the building envelope, allowing water to enter the building shell (walls, windows, roof, skylights, and other design features) and leading to rot, rust, decay, and mould. The syndrome is limited to the coastal climate area of British Columbia, particularly Greater Vancouver, the Fraser Valley, Victoria, and other parts of Vancouver Island. The problem has affected many condominiums and detached homes, and even some schools and hospitals. British Columbia's Homeowner Protection Office estimates that there are approximately 65,000 dwellings in the province that are "leaky condos."

Until the collapse of BC's New Home Warranty Program in 1998, many real estate agents and others believed that the warranty company would repair most building envelope failures. However, only a small percentage of problems were resolved by the warranty provider. In most cases, the homeowner was faced with having to pay for the repairs, which on average cost from $25,000 to $60,000 per unit, and in some cases as much as $150,000. Some leaky condo owners lost much or all of their life savings, even their homes. Family life, home-based businesses, and health all suffered from the financial strain, the disruption, and the mess during repairs.

The leaky condo crisis put a serious dent in the homebuyer market, especially in the Vancouver and Victoria areas. Before the syndrome was well documented, many buyers inadvertently bought homes that turned out to have building envelope problems. Once the problem was identified, they were unable to sell their homes, or had to do so at a huge financial loss.

Although sellers have a duty to disclose any problems related to building envelopes in a property disclosure statement, buyers cannot rely solely on this document. For this reason, it is extremely important for buyers to also scrutinize strata council meeting minutes, annual reports, building envelope reports, and Form "B" or estoppel certificates. When reading strata corporation minutes, buyers should check whether owners or tenants have complained of water coming through window frames, balconies, the roof, or any exposed part of the building. If you are buying a recently constructed building, you might want to check the developer's and builder's credentials and their other developments in the community, and find out about associations to which they belong, years of experience, certification, track record, and so on.

Further, ask whether the building's strata council is active in maintaining the building and the property. Is it responding to problems immediately? Is there enough money in the council's contingency or reserve fund to do repairs and improvements? What about the management company: Is it professional and reliable? Is the building self-managed? Are all the issues regarding repairs being dealt with? Also find out how many units are in the building. The more units in the building, the less each owner would have to pay if a special assessment were to be made to pay for major repairs.

As the buyer of a recreational home, you must assess whether the property you are interested in may have water ingress problems and whether the risk is too great for you to proceed with the purchase.

## What is a special assessment?

A special assessment is the outcome of a specially convened meeting of condominium unit owners who have an extraordinary expense that was not budgeted for in the regular maintenance fees and that cannot be fully covered by the monies in the contingency fund. Special assessments are generally rendered by the condominium corporation to pay for major improvements to the complex such as fixing the roof or repairing the parking garage. They are divided proportionally among the individual units. The amount assessed covers the shortfall and is charged pro rata (based on the unit entitlement of each strata owner).

If a special assessment is forthcoming, you will want to find out who will pay for it. If it is made during the time that the seller is still the owner and the assessment is levied before the completion date, even if the work is to be done after the proposed completion date, it should be stated in the contract of purchase and sale that the seller is responsible for paying the assessment.

If a special assessment is levied after the completion date, including special assessments that are proposed but not approved, the buyer will pay for this assessment. This detail must be written into the contract of purchase and sale to ensure that there is no misunderstanding between the parties later. If it is known that a special assessment will occur after possession, the unit's price might be drastically reduced to reflect that the buyer is taking on the responsibility of paying for the special assessment. Insurance coverage is available for special assessments. This type of insurance policy may be a very prudent investment.

## Beware of Buying a Former "Grow House"

A "grow house" or "grow-op" is a building that is or was used to grow marijuana. Police estimate that there are more than 50,000 active grow-ops in Canada today, and this number continues to increase. No community is immune from these marijuana-growing operations. They exist in almost every province and territory in Canada, from the largest urban centres to the smallest rural communities, in both residential and recreational homes. This problem is reaching epidemic proportions, especially in British Columbia, Ontario, and Quebec, and is often associated with money laundering.

Grow operations range in size from a one-bedroom basement to something as large as a barn or warehouse. Properties that are remote from much traffic and regular police scrutiny are particularly attractive to grow-op operators. Look for the following signs that may indicate a former grow house:

- Mould in corners where the walls and ceilings meet
- Roof vents
- Painted concrete floors in the basement with circular marks of where pots once stood
- Evidence of tampering with the electric meter (damaged or broken seals) or the ground around it
- Concrete masonry patches or alterations on the inside of the garage
- Patterns of screw holes on the walls
- Alteration of fireplaces
- Dented front doors (from police ramming the door)

If you are considering buying a property that you suspect may have once been a former grow house, it is likely that extensive cleaning and repair will be required. You may also want to speak to a specialist about the long-term health effects and risks of living in such a place.

As discussed in the section on mould issues below, you may need to hire a specialist to make sure there is no serious structural damage caused by high humidity and mould. Moisture can penetrate walls, ceilings, and the roof, and may require very expensive repairs. If this is the case, getting a detailed inspection report on the damage would be a good idea.

If you even suspect that the property you are purchasing could once have been a grow house, make sure that the issue is addressed in the property condition disclosure statement from the seller. Speak to the owners if they are present. It is your right as a buyer to ask the seller and/or owner about this concern and get the answers in writing. If you decide to proceed with buying such a property, you may want to negotiate a reduced price.

## Mould Issues

Mould results from too much humidity, poor ventilation systems, and/or wet construction materials. If mould is not removed, it can lead to wood rot and structural damage, and in moist climates such as BC and Ontario, this can be a serious problem for homeowners. Mould is blamed for a number of health issues, including breathing difficulties, headaches, nausea, skin rashes, and gastrointestinal ailments.

To protect yourself against buying a recreational home with mould problems, make sure you get a comprehensive home inspection done before finalizing the purchase. Mould damage has led many insurance companies to stop offering mould coverage in their property and liability policies. For example in Ontario, insurers only offer mould coverage under a separate environmental insurance policy. The premium for this environmental insurance is quite high for property owners — about $10,000 for $1 million coverage.

If you suspect the presence of mould in a recreational home, you may simply want to walk away from this property.

## Precautions When Using Wood Heating

Wood heating in cottages, such as with a wood stove or fireplace, can be cheaper than heating with electricity, plus it has a distinct aesthetic appeal during crisp fall evenings or snowy winter nights. If you have wood heating in your recreational home, make sure that you have working carbon monoxide detectors and smoke detectors on all floors of your cottage. In addition, you may want to ask the recreational-home inspector to check if the wood heater has been installed properly. Make sure you first ask the inspector if he or she is qualified to do such an inspection, as most inspectors are not specialized enough to check wood heating. However, they may be able to refer you to a specialist. Also note that if you intend to install a wood-heating appliance such as a new chimney, or replace one wood stove with another, many municipalities require a building permit.

Don't forget to inform your insurance company or broker whenever any change is made to the wood heating system. This includes adding or changing a wood stove, modifying a chimney, or any alteration that may influence the safety of the wood-heating system. Making the wood-heating system as safe as possible will give you the lowest possible premium for insurance coverage.

Contact the local fire department, recreational-home inspector, wood-heating retailer, and a local chimney sweep for fire safety information.

# Potential Problems with Oil Tanks

Many underground oil storage tanks in Canada have reached the end of their useful lives and are beginning to corrode, rust, and leak. It is a recreational property owner's legal responsibility to properly maintain the oil tank and clean up any spills or leaks that may occur. Leaking fuel oil tanks may create several hazards. Oil and its vapours can —

- generate a potentially explosive mixture,
- enter surface water,
- enter drinking water, and
- contaminate surrounding soil.

## How can you know whether an underground oil tank is leaking?

It is very difficult to detect a leaking underground oil tank if it has not been in use for some time. Some underground tanks may leak for years without owners realizing it. If oil consumption suddenly goes up and the oil tank is in use, the tank may have sprung a large leak. Call the fuel supplier for help in finding companies that will test underground tanks.

## Provincial and territorial standards for oil tanks

According to the Insurance Bureau of Canada, a recreational home with an exterior oil tank older than 15 years or an interior tank older than 25 years will not be insured. Most provinces and territories currently have safety standards for oil tanks. If you are considering buying a recreational home with an oil tank, check with the local government office for more information on oil tank safety standards.

# Electric Wiring Issues

According to a report from the Canadian Real Estate Association, some insurers are refusing to cover or renew policies on residential properties with 60 amp electricity, aluminum wiring, or knob and tube wiring. Knob and tube wiring, also known as open wiring, was used in homes in Canada for almost 50 years. If it was installed properly, it can provide many years of service. However, if the recreational home you are considering has knob and tube wiring, there are some guidelines that you need to follow:

- Get a qualified electrical contractor to check the knob and tube conductors for signs of deterioration and damage. If they may need replacement, get an estimate of the cost.

- Ask for a specific electrical contractor report, as some insurance companies may require this.
- Check the general inspection report to see if any electrical safety concerns are identified.

Speak to your professional recreational-home inspector for guidance and for more information. In addition, make certain that your contract allows for a subject condition allowing for approval of insurance for a property with aluminum electric wiring.

Recreational Property for Sale!

For Sale by Owner!

SOLD

Chapter 8

# BUILDING A RECREATIONAL HOME, AND OTHER OPTIONS

There are many pros and cons to building your own recreational home. If you start from scratch, everything can be built to your taste, but building a home is not without its challenges. First of all, unlike when building a residential home in the city, you would probably require the services of a general contractor or builder to oversee the project, as you would not likely be on-site to oversee each step. If you need to commute to your recreational property on a weekly basis during its construction, you may find this time-consuming, and eventually tiresome and expensive.

On the other hand, buying a resale home can also have challenges. Some homes may have been seriously neglected; they may have plumbing and electrical systems that are failing and need upgrading, or the roof may need replacing. Sometimes the damage is so severe that tearing down the building and starting over is the best option. You need to weigh the pros and cons of each situation before you come to the major decision of building or rebuilding your recreational property.

## Can You Build on Your Property?

The construction of your home must meet basic health, safety, and structural requirements as set out by the building code for the municipality. There is a permit process that makes sure your plans are in line with municipal requirements and zoning regulations. Before building on your property, make sure that it is not in a designated agricultural or forest reserve, as these zonings strictly limit what may or may not be built on a property. In British Columbia, for example, the Agricultural Land Reserve (ALR) is a provincial zone in which agriculture is recognized as the priority use. Farming is encouraged and non-agricultural uses are controlled.

As a homeowner, you are legally responsible for obtaining any building permits required. Some municipalities require a letter of authorization before your builder or contractor can apply for a permit on your behalf. When signing a contract with a builder, be sure to specify which permits are required and who will obtain them.

# Location

As touched upon in the preceding chapters, the first step is finding the property that is right for you. You've considered the following questions:

- Is the size of the land suitable for your recreational needs?
- Will you be able to access the land easily and cost-effectively?
- Is there a sewage disposal system ready to use?
- Are there waterlines available or an existing well?
- Is the grade reasonable, or is it too steep to build a home?
- Will you need to clear the land of trees before you begin building?

Each person's idea of a vacation or recreational home will differ, and you need to determine what type of terrain is ideal for you. People who make their purchase in the spring and summer may not realize how difficult it is to access the property in the middle of winter, with poor winter conditions such as heavy rain or blinding snow. Taking a boat ride to get to the recreational home in the summer is very different from taking the same boat ride in the winter, so you may want to visit the potential site during all seasons.

Equally important is where to build your recreational home on the property. You will need to consider the distance to the neighbours' homes (either too far or too close), wind patterns, light patterns, power and telephone hookups, the sewage system, water wells, and natural habitat. Always call a professional to help you find the best location on your property to build your home — architects and designers are worth consulting.

# Estimating Costs

When you have found your ideal parcel of land, you will need to create a blueprint of your recreational home. The blueprint will specify the design and square footage of the home to be built. If you take your blueprint to a builder or contractor, he or she can give you an estimate based on dollars per square foot. Once you have an idea of the cost, you can look into financing.

The cost of construction depends on a variety of factors, and local builders are the best source for information. Many local builders will already have building option packages and budgeting packages that you may want to consider. Costs can depend on size, type of structure, materials (e.g., local or imported, easily available or specially ordered), quality, and the time involved.

When considering the cost of labour, you will have to decide how skilled you want them to be — the more skilled the labourer, the more expensive the overall costs. Some skilled labourers may even need to be "flown in" for a special job.

Don't forget about the costs of transporting labourers and/or materials. If your property is hard to access — for example, if you can only reach your property by boat — you will definitely incur extra shipping and transportation expenses. Always ask your contractor or developer to give you a written estimate.

Once the building project is well underway, alterations to the original plan can incur extra costs. A simple alteration or upgrade may initially appear to be only a minor setback or a slight additional cost, but it may require extra permits, more time, more delays, and ultimately, more money. If any changes to the plans are necessary during construction, make sure you get the costs for these changes in writing before the builder proceeds with the alterations.

# Financing

Buying raw land with the intention of building on it may become a challenge when it comes time to acquiring financing. Typically, most banks will not finance vacant land. An option would be to refinance your residential home by way of obtaining a second mortgage from the equity in your home.

If you are able to buy the land but you need money for building a recreational home, you may be able to acquire a Construction Loan Mortgage, which is a short-term loan that will cover the costs of construction. Once the construction is complete, you will then need to apply for a long-term loan to pay for the construction loan. The lending institution will require you to submit the blueprint and the specifications for the recreational home along with the estimate of the construction costs (signed by the builder). The lender may also request a recent land survey, a copy of the deed, and a written document stating that the property is not mortgaged.

If you are buying property along with a pre-fab home, it is possible that financing options can be obtained through national lenders who are familiar with prefab homes. The lenders may provide this service based on an established history with a prefab-home company and the home's appraised value upon completion. This is not always the case, so do your research.

# The Builder
## Finding and hiring a builder

Finding and hiring a builder can be done by either talking to local homeowners or by contacting various associations in the area such as the Better Business Bureau or a home builders' association. An interview process can help you determine which builder to go with. Take the opportunity to ask all sorts of questions, particularly those about your major concerns — reliability, communication skills, work efficiency, and so on — and find out about the builder's past clients, his or her references, and what associations the builder belongs to.

If you are not impressed with the local builders — or if none are available when you want to build — you may decide to hire a builder from another location. Bringing somebody in to do the job can be expensive due to travel costs, but in the end it may be more expensive to hire someone local who isn't capable of meeting your expectations.

## Communicating with your builder

Determining exactly what you want and communicating this to your builder is extremely important. Writing these ideas in the form of a letter and/or contract is ideal. Words, drawings, and photos can be important ways to communicate effectively with the builder. A clear definition of the types of materials to be used — for example, size of planks and colour scheme — should be included in the contract. In addition, the method of payment must be determined in advance. Some contractors will require an advance payment for purchasing supplies; others will require a weekly or monthly payment.

You should ask the builder for a breakdown of the costs. Do the costs cover supplies and the transportation of the supplies? Are supplies to be billed every 30, 60, or 90 days, but the labour billed sooner? Will there be a discount from the supplier if the materials are paid for in less than 30 days? If so, how much will the discount amount to?

You must make sure everything is clarified in advance so there are not problems later on. If you do not understand something, ask until you do understand and get the answer in writing. The contract with the builder should include as much information as possible so there is no mistaking what services are being offered, and for what cost. You may want to hire a lawyer to review the contract. The following list outlines some of the important things the contract should cover:

- Hourly rates
- Cost and specifications of materials
- Start and completion date
- Contractor's management fee
- Construction and payment schedule
- Subcontractor/subtrade fees
- Payment holdbacks
- Builder's warranty
- Building permits
- Workers' compensation premiums

If you are working with any tradespeople, make sure that they carry workers' compensation and liability insurance and are fully bonded. Conduct your due diligence by asking them for a copy of their WCB insurance papers.

## Overseeing the progress

Overseeing the construction of your recreational home from beginning to end is very important. Be close by, or at the very least visit on a weekly basis to check up on tradespeople, suppliers, deliveries, and so on. If the project is falling behind, you will know because you are keeping a close eye on the progress. The further it falls behind, the more money it could end up costing you.

## Preparing the Land

Before any construction can take place, the boundaries of your property must be clearly marked. If there are no boundaries marked with stakes or pegs, you should hire a surveyor to do this for you. If you do not hire a professional and only mark approximate boundaries, you will risk having the city or municipality demolish a part of your building should you later find out the land actually belongs to your neighbour!

If your property happens to have trees in the exact area where you want to build your recreational home, you will need to find out the costs for clearing the trees. Some homeowners opt to sell the timber to cover clearing costs. If your timber isn't sellable, then you will have to calculate the cost of renting heavy equipment as well as hiring a skilled labourer to operate this equipment to remove the timber. Keep in mind that many areas restrict burning your timber.

You may also have to build an access road or driveway, if one does not exist. Depending on the size and the terrain, slope, and material to be used, this can be a major investment in itself, and permits can be required.

## Power and telephone lines

Will power lines and telephone lines be in place before construction is to take place, or will there be a need for a generator to provide power? Discuss these issues with your builder, as a temporary power panel may be set up during the construction process and a more permanent structure set up after construction is complete. If there are already homes in the area that are connected to power lines, you may be able to temporarily get power to your property, though costs may be substantial.

## Water and sewage

In addition, you will have to think beforehand about water supply and a sewage disposal system for use during construction. You may need to arrange to have a well dug so that there is water for cement, masonry, and plastering. If you want to delay drilling a well, as it can be very expensive, find out about other options such as cisterns for water deliveries.

## Building Inspectors and Municipal Inspectors

Obtain the services of a qualified inspector who will be able to help you with the construction of your recreational home. Many are specialized and have previous electrical or plumbing backgrounds, while others are generalists. Inspectors are unregulated in most provinces, so you should inquire about the inspector's credentials, ask for references, and ensure that the inspector has Errors and Omissions Insurance so that if you buy a home that requires a costly repair that the inspector didn't report, he or she can be held financially responsible for the cost of the repair.

City or municipal inspectors must inspect your recreational home at different stages to make sure it complies with the building codes of the jurisdiction where the property is located. Your contractor will deal with these inspectors as needed. If your property is in a remote area, it can sometimes take weeks for a municipal inspector to become available.

# Alternatives to Building a Recreational Home

## Prefab homes

An alternative to building a recreational home from the ground up would be purchasing a prefab home, which is pre-assembled to some degree before it is delivered to a property. Prefab homes can be cabins, cottages, or single-family dwellings. You can choose from a variety of plans, adjust the specifications to meet your needs, and then order the package and have it delivered. Many property developers are now providing joint-venture projects with manufacturers of prefab homes, making this option for a recreational home more attractive.

Once you have decided on the plans for your prefab home, you need to decide what stage of completeness you would like the prefab home to be in when it is delivered. You may need to hire a general contractor to oversee the site preparation (pouring the foundation and setting up water and sewage systems), assembly, and finishing of the prefab home. If you have building experience and feel confident in overseeing the project, it is possible you can do it yourself using the manual that is provided.

In terms of costs, there are many variables when purchasing a prefab home. You may buy a shell that you will need to fill in with the interior construction, electrical wiring, plumbing, etc., or the package you buy may include interior finishing. To find out more about costs, discuss the project in detail with the prefab-home company. Once you have decided how complete the home will be when delivered, you must talk to a local contractor to figure out additional costs.

The bonus of ordering a prefab home is that there is minimal land disruption, that is, very little waste and destruction to the property, and reduced on-site construction time. Most prefabs are considered an energy-efficient type of housing. They are built in an eco-friendly manner using heat-recovery systems and insulation systems that won't mould.

The cost of prefab homes can range from $125 to $200 per square foot. However, as prefab recreational homes become more popular, the prices are likely to decrease, making them more affordable. A mind-boggling array of stylish modernist prefabs is now available, including designs delivered complete to the site via trailer or tugboat, flat-packed house kits, collapsible studios that can be moved via SUV, and portable penthouses built to be flown from city rooftop to the country via helicopter. Search for "prefab homes" on the web for the latest designs, prices, and delivery options.

## Camping on your land

Another alternative to building is camping on your land, which may include staying in a motorhome or RV, or roughing it by setting up a tent on the land. In this case, you may want to build temporary structures such as a shed or an outhouse, but check local municipal guidelines before building. You may also want to inquire about local zoning laws and if there are any restrictions against temporary structures.

# Chapter 9
# BUYING RECREATIONAL PROPERTY AS AN INVESTMENT

Buying a recreational property as a potential investment means you will likely do one of three things with it: you may "flip" the property, rent it out, or hold it until the land value increases and then sell it. Flipping is when a person buys a property for the sole purpose of reselling it quickly for a profit. Some people find good deals on recreational homes that are in foreclosure or under construction, while others buy a recreational home that can be remodelled quickly and efficiently and then put on the market with a huge markup. If you choose to remodel a recreational home that you plan to sell right away, you must make sure that the remodelling budget doesn't get out of control because you are not building your dream recreational home, you are just improving it enough to make a reasonable profit. When you put the recreational home back on the market, the price you list it for will depend on the current market rates. Always consider the financial risk of not being able to sell right away if the market slows down.

Buying a property for the sole purpose of renting it out can be lucrative as well. The income can help pay down your mortgage and contribute to maintenance costs, utilities, insurance, and so on. Check zoning laws in the area to make sure that you are able to rent out the property. If you are not in the area all the time, you may need to hire someone to look after maintenance, and perhaps to look after rental bookings.

A property with investment potential will mean different things to different people. What are you interested in and what is your risk level?

## Determining Investment Potential

Discuss a recreational property's investment potential with your agent. Each area and each property is unique. For example, investment potential in Whistler, BC, will be different from investment potential in rural Nova Scotia. An agent may also help you locate an area that is becoming popular, which means the demand for the recreational property will eventually exceed the supply.

# The Importance of Location

When considering recreational property to rent or to sell, keep in mind that location means different things to different people. For example, a skier's ideal location would be something that is truly a ski-in/ski-out condo or a cabin that has views of the slopes and mountains. For others, a residential property in the middle of a golf course resort is ideal. Location is something very personal. Think about where buyers or renters want their recreational home.

Properties that are near or adjacent to a body of water such as a lake, ocean, or river are popular, including many resort-style hotel condos. Typically, a single-detached home or cabin by the ocean will get better sales results because the demand for ocean and water views is high and this type of property is limited. Consider this when buying property for investment.

## Accessibility

Accessibility is important because most recreational property renters and purchasers are looking for property that is located within several hours' drive of their primary residence, making weekend trips possible. A lot of recreational-home buyers do not want to experience the inconvenience and cost of a long trip to get to their recreational home. However, a unique recreational home in a hard-to-get-to location may be exactly what some out-of-country buyers are seeking.

You may also want to consider proximity to the United States, because recreational real estate close to the border makes it attractive to American buyers and renters.

## Exposure through events and films

Major events, whether they are anticipated or have already taken place, play an important role in recreational real estate. After Expo '86 in Vancouver, real estate sales in regions within several hours of Vancouver increased steadily. With the upcoming 2010 Winter Olympics, real estate sales are expected to continue to rise in the BC Lower Mainland and around Whistler. Likewise, the film industry has played an important role in generating real estate sales, especially in Ontario, Manitoba, Alberta, and British Columbia.

## Recreational activities

The recreational market is catering to a wider demographic of people, including the generation after baby boomers, who have young families. It is important to explore what a recreational property can offer to these buyers and renters. If you are thinking about people's recreational hobbies, there are endless possibilities: skiing, kayaking, golfing, canoeing, mountain climbing, snowmobiling, hunting, fishing and fly fishing, dirt biking, skydiving, hiking, scuba diving, and so much more. It is important to determine what is popular with recreational buyers and renters and to consider the different amenities that a recreational property can offer.

Determing what type of buyer you are targeting and what lifestyle you are marketing. This will affect what would be an ideal investment property for you: a condo by the beach, a detached home in a residential area, or a chalet or condo at a ski resort.

## Increasing the Property Value

Increasing a property's value will depend on the local market. Fixing access roads, improving the water supply system, and renovating typically increase a property's value. Ask your agent for guidance on how to increase your property's value and how to get a positive return on your investment. For example, a hot tub or sauna is a welcome feature after a day on the slopes and a great place to relax with family and friends. Hot tubs and saunas will certainly add to the resale value of a recreational ski property but for other properties — especially where there is a water shortage — such additions may yield a negative return on the investment.

Ski chalets that offer unique luxury features have great resale potential. For example, a steam shower, granite countertops, ski-to-door access, exceptional views, floor-to-ceiling rock fireplaces, cathedral ceilings, and an open-plan kitchen or a kitchen with a breakfast bar or island all help ensure maximum resale value. Ask your agent for other ways to increase your property's value so you can get positive rates of return for your investment property.

# Chapter 10

# NON-RESIDENTS: BUYING AND SELLING RECREATIONAL PROPERTY

## Can Non-Residents Buy Real Estate in Canada?

At present, in most situations non-residents can purchase real estate in Canada. Second homes and recreational properties are owned by many non-residents, primarily people from the US but also from Asia and Europe. However, there are restrictions for buying agricultural land in British Columbia, Saskatchewan, and Manitoba. You need to be a resident, living in Canada at least 183 days per year if you wish to buy agricultural land, although some exemptions are granted.

Issues concerning non-residency are typically addressed in the agreement of purchase and sale; they can vary by provincial jurisdiction. Expert advice is recommended on all matters relating to non-resident ownership. If English is not your first language, retain a professional translator to help you understand the intricacies of the real estate transaction.

## Canadian currency

If you are a non-resident purchasing property in Canada, you must exchange your currency for Canadian currency. When making an offer, funds for a down payment, a stakeholder, or for the final purchase must be received by specified times. To expedite the transfer of funds, secure funds, and provide the best currency exchange, you are advised to use a customs brokerage house. Ask your real estate agent to recommend a list of foreign customs brokers.

## Can non-residents obtain financing to purchase recreational property?

Many Canadian lenders provide mortgages to non-residents. These lenders will generally finance up to a maximum of 65 percent of the purchase price or appraised value, whichever is lower. The following list outlines some of the documentation that lenders may require:

- Appraisal by a qualified, bank-approved appraiser
- Proof of down payment
- Credit bureau information from the buyer's country of origin
- Reference letter from a bank in the buyer's country of origin

To facilitate making payments on the mortgage, it is a good idea to open a Canadian dollar bank account in Canada.

## Down payment

Lenders generally consider mortgages to non-residents as higher risk than resident mortgages. The increased risk is compensated by either having a larger down payment or a higher interest rate. To access the best interest rates, borrowers are typically required to have a 35 percent down payment.

If you have a down payment of between 25 percent and 35 percent, some non-traditional lenders are willing to provide financing. These lenders, who do not follow the standard lending guidelines, would lend to individuals who do not qualify at banks or credit unions. Expect the interest rate to be higher than with traditional financing.

## Residents of the United States

American residents have an advantage over residents from other countries when it comes to purchasing real estate in Canada. For one thing, mortgage brokers can access US credit bureaus to obtain credit histories. As well, many mortgage brokers have a relationship with US-based lenders. US lenders are able to provide up to 90 percent financing for an owner-occupied residence and 85 percent financing for non-owner occupied properties such as vacation homes and rentals.

## Can a Non-Resident Reside in Canada, and for How Long?

According to Citizenship and Immigration Canada, all visitors admitted to Canada will be permitted to stay for a maximum of six months, unless otherwise notified in writing by an examining officer at point of entry.

If you are buying recreational property and wish to live in Canada for longer periods than a visitor's visa allows, you should contact the nearest Canadian embassy. If you are already in Canada, contact Citizenship and Immigration Canada. The government website, www.cic.gc.ca/english/immigrate/index.html, provides information about applying for permanent resident status, which gives non-Canadians the right to live in Canada. Permanent residents enjoy most of the rights and responsibilities of Canadian citizens, but they must meet certain residency obligations to maintain their status. Like Canadian citizens, permanent residents enjoy all the rights guaranteed under the Canadian Charter of Rights and Freedoms, such as equality rights, legal rights, mobility rights, freedom of religion, freedom of expression, and freedom of association.

## Taxes

If you are a non-resident of Canada considering buying recreational real estate in Canada, be sure to read Chapter 5, which addresses tax issues.

### Residence status and income tax

If non-residents stay in Canada for more than 182 consecutive days, they may be considered Canadian residents for Canadian income tax purposes. Canada has tax treaties with many countries — treaties designed to avoid double taxation for people who would otherwise pay tax on the same income in two countries. For more information, log on to Canada Revenue Agency's website at www.cra-arc.gc.ca or consult a qualified tax consultant who specializes in non-resident taxes.

# Important Information for a Non-Resident Selling a Recreational Home

Non-residents who dispose of Canadian real estate must notify the Canadian government within ten days of the date the property was disposed of by completing the form "Request by a Non-Resident of Canada for a Certificate of Compliance Related to the Disposition of Taxable Canadian Property." This form is issued by the Canada Revenue Agency (CRA) and can be found online in the forms and publications section of CRA's website at www.cra-arc.gc.ca. The Certificate of Compliance will be issued to you when the CRA has either received a prepayment on the taxes you owe or an appropriate security payment. If you do not notify the government within ten days of the sale, you may be fined.

# PART 2
## PROCEEDING WITH THE PURCHASE

# Chapter 11
# MAKING AN OFFER

Once you have found the property you would like to purchase — the one that meets most of your requirements for a recreational home — a written offer to purchase must be prepared. Given the substantial nature of your investment, you are advised to work with a lawyer or an agent in preparing an offer to purchase. An offer is usually recorded on a standard form called a contract of purchase and sale; in some provinces and territories, this form is called an agreement of purchase and sale. Terms, conditions, changes, and any other additions are written in an addendum.

## What to Look for When Viewing Properties

Gather as much information as possible to determine whether you want to place an offer on a property. You can carry out a preliminary, informal investigation of the property before placing an offer, and a more formal investigation after placing an offer. Things to investigate include seller's motivation; prior offers for the property; condition of the property; the moving dates; any restrictions; and health, safety, and environmental concerns.

## Seller's motivation

If the seller has already moved out of the home, he or she may be eager to sell the property, and this could be to your advantage.

## Prior offers

Try to find out if there have been any offers in the past, the details of what happened, or why a deal may have collapsed. If it collapsed because the buyers did not get financing, you might want to ask if the financing problems stemmed from the property itself or from the buyer. For example, a bank may have refused to finance a condominium unit because the building had problems in the past. In this case, your agent may be able to find out if there are other lending institutions that have recently financed other units in the same building; or, given this information, you may opt not to proceed with an offer.

If the deal collapsed because of a negative report from a home or building inspection, find out what those deficiencies or defects were. It may be a waste of time to proceed any further, or those deficiencies or defects may be minor and you may still want to proceed. **Note:** You may be able to obtain a copy of the home inspection report, but you may need to pay for a portion of its cost. Ask your agent about this if you are seriously considering making an offer on a property.

# Property condition

Prior to getting an inspection from a certified home inspector, you will probably conduct a preliminary assessment of the property condition. The following are points to look for:

- *Exterior condition:* Look at the condition of the roof, brick, mortar, paint, siding, decks, and patios.
- *Energy efficiency:* Ask about the type of heating and insulation used. Is the entire building insulated, and if so, with what types of insulation? Some types are more energy-efficient than others, and some, such as urea formaldehyde foam insulation (UFFI), may result in health problems such as irritation to eyes, nose, and throat; cough or respiratory distress; nausea; headaches; and dizziness. Testing has shown that UFFI installed in 1980 or earlier should not cause excess indoor exposure to formaldehyde today, unless it comes in contact with water or moisture. (Wet or deteriorating UFFI should be removed by a specialist and the source of the moisture ingress repaired.)
- *Air quality:* Check for the conditions and materials that will maintain a healthy indoor environment. Does the house smell clean and fresh? In basements and crawl spaces, look for mould, water stains, and leaks. If you happen to see a humidifier or dehumidifier in the home, this may indicate that the home has either too much moisture or not enough moisture.
- *Structural problems:* Ensure that doors and windows don't stick and that floors are level. Doors and windows that don't open easily and uneven floors may indicate structural problems.
- *Water pressure:* Turn on taps to see what the water pressure is like, and flush the toilet to see if the water is running and that the toilet and taps are working properly.
- *Parking:* Determine whether the building has a private or shared driveway or parking space.
- *Efflorescence:* Efflorescence is a crystalline deposit on the face of a stone or brick wall. Damage to masonry may result from the growth of salt crystals near its surface. Possible causes include the masonry materials, the mortar, the backing, and "outside" contaminants such as groundwater.

Some sellers may be willing to arrange for minor repairs or minor improvements, such as painting the interior or installing new carpets. Other sellers may accept a price reduction in lieu of making such improvements. Some may sell the home on an "as is" basis.

## Property condition disclosure statement

A property condition disclosure statement (PCDS) is an important tool for all homebuyers, and for all types of property. It provides both a history of the property and a description of the condition of the property, which is documented in writing, signed by the seller and buyer, and dated. The PCDS is a great tool because it deals with structural, mechanical, and environmental issues, including information on plumbing, sewage systems, and renovations. It also provides the seller with written proof that deficiencies or defects were disclosed and the buyer was made aware of them. (See Sample 3.)

The intent of a PCDS is to properly document information so that the buyer can make an informed decision. Unfortunately, a PCDS that is filled out and signed by an owner who has been renting out the property is not as accurate as one provided by an owner who has actually occupied the property. An absent landlord may not be aware of some of the problems with the property.

A PCDS should be current and accurate. The listing agent should confirm the statement's facts by, for example, ascertaining when renovations or improvements were done and whether they passed inspection. If the seller states that the roof shingles were replaced two years ago, the listing agent should check the date by asking for a copy of the invoice or contacting the roofer. Some home inspectors read a PCDS and may take the time to verify or deny what has been written. You should review the PCDS prior to making an offer, or you can make an offer subject to receiving and approving a PCDS within a specified time.

Some real estate boards and associations have made the completion of the form mandatory for every listing. They refuse to process a listing through their MLS systems until the completed form has been submitted. Many provinces and municipalities have their own PCDS forms; these vary from one area to another. Contact your local real estate board for these forms.

If you are unable to obtain a PCDS, you may do one of two things: walk away because the owner has refused to provide crucial information to you, or hire a qualified property inspector to give you a detailed assessment.

**Note:** In some municipalities, such as west of Edmonton, there is no property condition disclosure statement required; however, buyers still can request one from sellers.

# What Should the Offer to Purchase Include?

As the buyer, you are the "author" of the offer to purchase. You decide on the price you would like to offer, the length of time your offer is valid, how much of a deposit and down payment you would like to make, and the dates you would like to complete the sale and take possession. Although your agent can assist in writing up the contract, it is you who ultimately decides the terms and conditions for your offer.

# Competing or Multiple Offers

In a seller's market, when many buyers are looking for the same type of property, or if the property that is being sold is a very good value, it is common to have more than one buyer place an offer to purchase on a property. When two parties make an offer to purchase, they have made competing offers. When more than two parties place an offer at the same time, the seller receives multiple offers.

When you are in this kind of situation, your agent will usually help you through the negotiation process. He or she will advise you of various tactics and strategies you can adopt, and outline the strengths and weaknesses of your offer.

As a homebuyer faced with a bidding war, you need to know the following:

- *This is not the time to lowball.* Put your best price on the table. When there are no other offers, a buyer can negotiate the price that is acceptable to both the buyer and the seller. In competing- and multiple-offer situations, the buyer competes with other buyers. Putting your best price at the beginning could give you the advantage. When you lowball sellers, you give the idea that you are going for a win-lose negotiation strategy, with the sellers as the losers.

## PROPERTY CONDITION DISCLOSURE STATEMENT

The Seller is responsible for disclosing to the buyer any and all material facts about the property. This form is intended to aid the Seller in this duty and to aid the Buyer in his or her evaluation of the property. The Seller is responsible for the accuracy of the information provided herein, and verifies that it is true to the best of his or her knowledge and complies with local regulations.

Date: _____

Address of property: _____

Seller must initial appropriate column

| | Yes | No | Don't know | N/A |
|---|---|---|---|---|
| 1. Is the property connected to a public sewer system? | [ ] | [ ] | [ ] | [ ] |
| 2. Is the property connected to a public water system? | [ ] | [ ] | [ ] | [ ] |
| 3. Does the water system have any known defects? | [ ] | [ ] | [ ] | [ ] |
| 4. Does the septic system have any known defects? | [ ] | [ ] | [ ] | [ ] |
| 5. Is the property connected to a private water system or serviced by a private well? | [ ] | [ ] | [ ] | [ ] |
| 6. Does the property now have or has it ever had an underground oil storage tank? | [ ] | [ ] | [ ] | [ ] |
| 7. Are there currently or have there ever been toxic substances stored on the property? | [ ] | [ ] | [ ] | [ ] |
| 8. Has the property ever contained asbestos insulation? | [ ] | [ ] | [ ] | [ ] |
| 9. Has the property ever contained formaldehyde insulation? | [ ] | [ ] | [ ] | [ ] |
| 10. Is the ceiling insulated? | [ ] | [ ] | [ ] | [ ] |
| 11. Are the exterior walls insulated? | [ ] | [ ] | [ ] | [ ] |
| 12. Are you aware of any structural defects of the premises? | [ ] | [ ] | [ ] | [ ] |
| 13. Are there problems with any of the following: | | | | |
|    * heating and/or air conditioning systems | [ ] | [ ] | [ ] | [ ] |
|    * fireplace(s) | [ ] | [ ] | [ ] | [ ] |
|    * electrical system | [ ] | [ ] | [ ] | [ ] |
|    * plumbing system | [ ] | [ ] | [ ] | [ ] |
|    * hot tub and/or swimming pool | [ ] | [ ] | [ ] | [ ] |
|    * rodents and/or insects | [ ] | [ ] | [ ] | [ ] |
|    * mould | [ ] | [ ] | [ ] | [ ] |
|    * leakage or moisture | [ ] | [ ] | [ ] | [ ] |
| 14. Are you aware of any damage due to fire, water, or wind? | [ ] | [ ] | [ ] | [ ] |
| 15. Has this house ever been used as a marijuana grow operation or a crystal meth laboratory? | [ ] | [ ] | [ ] | [ ] |
| 16. Does the roof leak or has it ever been damaged? | [ ] | [ ] | [ ] | [ ] |
| 17. How old is the roof? _____ years | [ ] | [ ] | [ ] | [ ] |
| 18. Has the property ever been flooded? | [ ] | [ ] | [ ] | [ ] |
| 19. Is the property subject to any easements, rights-of-way, or shared-use agreements? | [ ] | [ ] | [ ] | [ ] |
| 20. Have you received notice of any claim against the property? | [ ] | [ ] | [ ] | [ ] |
| 21. Are there any legal actions pending that may affect the property? | [ ] | [ ] | [ ] | [ ] |
| 22. Are you aware of any additions, alterations, or renovations made to the property? | [ ] | [ ] | [ ] | [ ] |
| 23. Has a final building inspection been approved or a final occupancy permit been obtained? | [ ] | [ ] | [ ] | [ ] |
| 24. Are there any disclosures not covered above? | [ ] | [ ] | [ ] | [ ] |

**Comments** (attach additional pages if necessary):

_____
_____
_____

| Additional clauses specific to strata/condo units | Yes | No | Don't know | N/A |
|---|---|---|---|---|
| 25. Are there any special assessments proposed or voted on? (If yes, provide information below.) | [ ] | [ ] | [ ] | [ ] |
| 26. Are there any restrictions regarding the following: | | | | |
|    * pets | [ ] | [ ] | [ ] | [ ] |
|    * rentals | [ ] | [ ] | [ ] | [ ] |
|    * age | [ ] | [ ] | [ ] | [ ] |
|    * TV antennas/satellite dishes | [ ] | [ ] | [ ] | [ ] |
|    * parking for guests | [ ] | [ ] | [ ] | [ ] |
| 27. Are the following documents available: | | | | |
|    * bylaws | [ ] | [ ] | [ ] | [ ] |
|    * current year operating budget | [ ] | [ ] | [ ] | [ ] |
|    * current year financial statements | [ ] | [ ] | [ ] | [ ] |
|    * strata council meeting minutes for last 12 months, including extraordinary meetings and AGM | [ ] | [ ] | [ ] | [ ] |
| 28. What is the monthly maintenance fee? $_____ | [ ] | [ ] | [ ] | [ ] |
| 29. Does unit come with parking stall? | [ ] | [ ] | [ ] | [ ] |
| 30. Does unit come with storage locker? | [ ] | [ ] | [ ] | [ ] |

**Comments** (attach additional pages if necessary):

_____
_____
_____

The Seller(s) acknowledges that the information provided on this form is true and complete to the best of his or her knowledge as of the date on page 1. Any additional information or amendments to the above information that may arise will be disclosed to the Buyer prior to closing. The Seller acknowledges receipt of a copy of this form and agrees that a copy may be provided to the Buyer.

_____    _____
*Seller's signature*         *Seller's signature*

_____    _____
*Print name*                *Print name*

The Buyer(s) acknowledges receipt of a copy of this form. The Buyer also acknowledges his or her own obligation to examine the property to verify all material facts, and that he or she should also have a property inspection done by a professional, independent third party.

_____    _____
*Buyer's signature*          *Buyer's signature*

_____    _____
*Print name*                *Print name*

This form is not intended as a warranty or guarantee of any kind.

- *Include a copy of the letter of commitment from the lending institution or have your financing pre-approved.* Doing so shows the seller that you have not only taken initiative and saved the seller time in researching your financing capabilities, but also that you are a serious buyer.

# Evaluating Recreational-Home Prices

To evaluate the price of a listed property, it is useful to know the general rules for how sellers price their homes. The most effective method for evaluating prices is to use a Comparative Market Analysis (CMA). Pricing per square foot is not particularly useful unless the property is less than one year old.

## How sellers price their homes

Listing agents who represent sellers base their price on homes that have recently sold in the neighbourhood, on pending sales, and on active and expired listings. Typically, the owner's asking price — the advertised price of the house — is slightly higher than fair market value and may include the cost of marketing the property and of the agent's services. FSBOs may also have asking prices that are higher than fair market value. Review a CMA before responding to such listings.

## Comparative Market Analysis

Before you place an offer, your agent will provide you with a Comparative Market Analysis, which involves collecting and analyzing market sales data for similar properties that have recently been sold. This approach assumes that the market value of a property is equal to the price recently paid for similar properties; it operates on the "principle of substitution." A CMA is prepared when a buyer is interested in a property and would like to receive as much information as

possible about it, including whether that property is priced within fair market value.

The CMA method is most useful for similar properties that are within the same property class, such as single-family dwellings or condominium units. Similar features might include comparable square footage, number of bedrooms and bathrooms, age, amenities, frontage and depth (for single-detached homes), etc. When a CMA is used for recreational properties, a comparison is made with active, sold, and expired listings in the same area with the same characteristics as the property being compared. That is, a single-detached home is compared with other single-detached homes in the same area, and not in another area (unless there is nothing nearby to compare it with). If, in a condominium, there are no other units that have recently been sold, comparisons are made with a unit in a similar building in the same area. In other words, apples are compared with other apples, and not oranges!

CMAS are calculated by looking through current listings and all of the properties that were sold in the previous six months to a year. Although a price range is given to document fair market value, this is not an exact science: each property is unique. One property could face south or east; another could have a view of the water, and so on. In addition, agents are not aware of all properties sold, especially those sold through private sales. A CMA has a time-limited value; pay attention to the date, because if it is even a month or two old, it may not reflect the present market.

Most lending institutions will require an appraisal of your selected property. Appraisers make their evaluation of what a recreational home is worth based on land values, the home's condition, etc. In general, appraisers tend to be on the conservative side when providing a value to a home, so the appraised value may differ from the purchase price that buyers are willing to pay at a given point in time. The appraised value may affect the amount of mortgage a bank will loan you.

## Comparing unique properties

When purchasing any type of recreational property, especially properties with unique features, it is more difficult to establish an accurate comparison than with urban residential homes. Comparing the same types of recreational properties may be hard to do because of the distance between them (no similar properties in the area) or because they have unique features, such as having only boat access. The best you can do is look for similar listings in comparable areas.

# Chapter 12
# REMOVING SUBJECTS

Your offer to purchase will most likely include a few subject clauses, also known as condition precedents, which specify the conditions that must be met before the transaction can be completed. The amount of time you will have to remove subjects must be agreed to by the seller. Although there is no set rule, if you have pre-qualified for a mortgage you might require ten business days to remove subjects. This can be a stressful time, as you have much information to gather in a short time.

## Subject Clauses

Subject clauses range from deposit clauses to financing clauses; your agent or legal representative will include the subject clauses that are appropriate to your situation. For example, a subject clause for financing means that the buyer will purchase the property provided that a third party, in this case a lender, approves the mortgage. Another example is a requirement for a building inspection. In this case, the third party is the building or home inspector who will provide a report, but you will decide whether the building passes the inspection and if that subject can be removed.

## Why do you include subject clauses in the contract?

You need to include subject clauses in your contract because most of the time, important documents such as copies of the title search or strata plan are not provided to you until you have made a written offer to purchase. By placing a subject clause, you are saying that although you are making an offer to purchase, you need to approve of the information provided on these documents. For example, most homebuyers need a mortgage. Placing an offer "subject to obtaining financing" means that you will purchase only if you obtain a mortgage from a financial institution. If you are unable to obtain financing, you are not able to meet this condition, and the contract collapses.

## The most common subject clauses

The most common subject clauses concern financing, building inspections, property condition disclosure statements, title searches, and, in strata corporations, the reviewing of two years' (or more) worth of minutes, viewing and approving a Form "B" or estoppel certificate, and reviewing the strata bylaws and strata plans. Your agent or legal representative will include subject clauses that are appropriate to your situation.

## What does it mean to remove subjects?

Once you have placed an offer on the table, you will perform due diligence by reviewing all relevant documents carefully, asking questions about the property, and having a professional building inspection performed on the property. Your agent will help you obtain the necessary information, as stipulated in the contract of purchase and sale or in your offer to purchase.

The most common subject clauses for single-detached homes concern these issues:

- Title search
- Financing
- Building or home inspection
- Property condition disclosure statement

The most common subject clauses for condominiums concern these issues:

- Title search
- Form "B" or estoppel certificate
- Engineer's report and building envelope report
- Minutes from the strata council meetings of the last two years
- Copy of strata council bylaws and house rules
- Minutes from annual general meetings and any extraordinary special meetings of the last two years

- Financial statements (latest approved balance sheet and income sheet)
- Property condition disclosure statement

Once you receive these documents, it is your responsibility to go over them carefully and to make your own inquiries. You may contact property managers, the president of the strata council, and others to obtain specific information. Always review the documents carefully so that you will be able to make an informed decision — one based on facts, rather than opinion or emotion.

After reading these documents, you will be able to determine whether or not to proceed with a building or home inspection. For condominium buyers, two years' worth of minutes should contain enough information for you to know about the history of the building. It may contain complaints by other owners or tenants regarding water leaks, building envelope failure, theft or vandalism, and other matters. If you decide that the minutes show no signs of problems with the building, proceed with the building inspection. Make the necessary arrangements and inform the agent about the scheduled appointment. If a tenant occupies the property, at least 24 hours' notice is typically required.

## How long do you have to remove subjects?

Give yourself enough time to perform the tasks outlined as subject clauses. Leaving the duties to the last minute may prevent you from doing the follow-up research that is essential in the decision-making process.

The rule of thumb regarding the deadline for subject removals is that it is a date that is agreed upon by both parties. Most subjects can be removed within ten business days. This should give you enough time to arrange financing, obtain documents that need to be ordered from the property management company, and hire a building or home inspector (this assumes that you have already lined up a legal representative, building inspector, and mortgage broker). It may be a good idea to get some time off work to focus on removing these subjects and making the necessary inquiries, so that you can make informed decisions. If you need more time to perform the tasks outlined in your contract of purchase and sale, an addendum noting the change in dates must be agreed to and signed by both parties.

While the subjects are being removed, the property is taken off the market. As a result, leaving the subject removal for more than two weeks may be unreasonable for the seller, and the seller might not agree to revise the subject removal dates stipulated in the contract of purchase and sale.

See the Subject Removal Checklist (Checklist 2) at the end of this chapter to help you move through the subject removal process.

# Recreational-Home Inspections
## What should an inspection include?

A building and home inspection is a thorough visual investigation and objective written assessment of the physical structure, heating, plumbing, and electrical systems, and all components of a property from the roof to the foundation. Some recreational-home inspectors include in the report how well built the home is, whether any repairs are necessary, and their estimated cost. The report may also note the priorities — what should get fixed first, and how soon it should be fixed.

You may find a recreational-home inspector by inquiring at a local professional association of home inspectors, by asking your real estate representative for recommendations, by seeking a referral from friends and family members, or by searching on the Internet. As mentioned in Chapter 8, building inspectors are unregulated in most provinces, so you should inquire about the inspector's credentials, ask for references, and

ensure that the inspector has Errors and Omissions Insurance. **Note:** An agent is not trained to inspect a home or a building, but you can ask your agent to recommend a list of qualified inspectors.

For older homes, you may also ask an inspector to check for the presence of termites, lead paint, asbestos, underground oil tanks, wood-heating devices, mould, or other such problems. The details of each building inspection depend on the municipality, the individual building inspector, and yourself.

Before you hire a building or home inspector, ask what services are provided and at what cost. Some inspectors prepare a written inspection report filled with comments and suggestions as well as photos for documentation.

## Cottage inspection

If you are purchasing a cottage, make sure that the inspector specializes in cottage homes and is familiar with their particularities such as winterization, septic tank issues, and so on. Many recreational properties are more exposed to the natural elements than urban dwellings are. You may want to refer to the Single-Detached Home Inspection section below, as cottage inspections will have many of the same aspects.

## Condominium inspection

If you are purchasing a condominium, make sure your inspector specializes in condominium inspections. The building inspector should look at the unit's plumbing and electrical systems, appliances, and all exposed areas such as balconies, patios, and decks. Depending on your budget, you can also ask the inspector to report on the electrical room, boiler room, roof, parking space or garage, and storage space, and in newer condominiums, on an air filtration system. Inspectors will also inspect common areas such as hallways, lobby areas, and stairways, if asked to do so. Some building inspectors will also read strata corporation minutes, property condition disclosure statements, building envelope reports, and engineering reports as applicable.

### What areas of a condominium may need repair?

Two areas of condominium property that may need repair are the interior common areas and the building envelope. The interior common areas are stairwells, hallways, lobby areas, and garages. A building envelope includes all the building components that separate the indoor conditioned space from the outdoor unconditioned space. Samples of building envelope include the exterior walls, foundations, roof, and outside windows and doors. A building envelope failure means that any or all of these areas have water ingress caused by wind, rain, and air pressure.

A building-envelope problem may exist if there are visual signs of wood rot or mould, peeling paint, cracked or missing sealants, water flowing down the sides of the building or water stains, pools of water on the decks with no drainage system, or windows that are wet on the inside. Further, when reading through the srata minutes, if there is no regular inspection and preventative maintenance program in place, this may be a sign of potential problems.

## Single-detached home inspection

A building inspection for a single-detached home will take longer, and cost more, than one that is done for a condominium. The following aspects are included:

- Roof
- Plumbing
- Wiring and electrical systems
- Furnace
- Hot water tanks

- Wood-heating systems, including wood stoves and fireplaces
- Gutters
- Decks
- Garages or carports
- Foundation
- Drainage
- Underground oil storage tanks
- Indoor storage tanks
- Security systems
- Ceilings and walls
- Septic tanks
- Mould
- Insulation (particularly for the presence of asbestos)
- Additions, renovations, upgrades to the home
- Damage due to wind, fire, or water, including moisture and water ingress in the walls, basement, or crawl space
- Infestation by insects or rodents
- Damage due to raccoons, squirrels, birds, or other wild animals

Ask the building inspector to also provide you with a "deficiency list" of things that need to be fixed before you would finalize the sale or before moving to the property.

## What if you don't want to have an inspection done?

A proper building inspection is the only way to fully determine the condition of the recreational property you are purchasing. A report can inform you about the deficiencies that you might want to address with the sellers. If you choose not to have an inspection done, your agent will ask you to sign an addendum stating that you have waived the right to the inspection.

## Can you get a relative or friend to do the inspection?

For your peace of mind, you can have a relative or friend inspect the recreational home, in addition to hiring a professional building inspector. But don't substitute those inspections for a professional inspection.

## An inspection for a remodelled property

If the recreational home you are purchasing has just been remodelled, it is still a good idea to have a professional building inspection done. You will want to ensure that every alteration has been done according to code and that the remodelling, especially if it was extensive, was done with the required building permit.

It is also a good idea to find out — and get in writing — exactly what has been remodelled. Did the seller him- or herself reshingle the roof? Is he or she a professional and qualified to do so? It would also be wise to ask the seller to provide you with invoices and bills to verify that the work and materials used in the renovation have been fully paid.

## The cost of the recreational-home inspection

Inspections vary in price. A recreational-home inspector's fees can range from $150 to $300 for a small home. Some inspectors charge on the basis of the number of square feet in the property. They may charge more if the property is in an outlying area. Others charge an hourly rate or base their fees on the type of inspection that you require.

Typically, the recreational-home inspector is paid after completing the inspection. Even if you decide, after hearing of all the deficiencies of the property, that you don't want to move forward with the purchase, you are still required to pay for the services of the inspector. Sometimes,

an inspector will charge you less for your next recreational-home inspection if you require one. However, it is always wise to ask an inspector about costs before hiring him or her.

## Can the agent pay for the recreational-home inspection?

Agents are advised not to pay the cost of the inspection report on behalf of buyers. This helps them avoid the possibility or even the appearance of a conflict of interest.

## When the home inspection fails

If an inspection fails, or if the recreational-home inspector notices a deficiency that you did not anticipate or are not able or willing to fix, you may decide not to remove this subject or condition precedent from the offer to purchase until the problem has been remedied. The inspection has failed and does not satisfy you, so the contract becomes void. You inform the agent about your decision and why you will not be able to remove that subject. A contract can be terminated if an issue cannot be resolved or the buyer is not satisfied with the results of the inspection. This is known as a non-fulfillment of a condition precedent.

If, however, you are still interested in purchasing the property despite a failed inspection and would like to renegotiate the price, you can inform your agent that you are still willing to buy the property, provided that either the price is reduced by the amount of the estimated repairs or the deficiencies are repaired by the seller. The seller can either accept or reject your offer.

When purchasing a property, it is important to distinguish between "curable" and "incurable" defects. Many recreational-home buyers find that fixing up a property is a great way to invest money while having a place to go for vacation — especially if the property's defects aren't too difficult or expensive to correct. These are curable defects, which include a new coat of paint, a little bit of landscaping, or a new carpet. Incurable defects might include serious structural problems. Know your limits, and make sure that you know exactly what you are getting into.

## Removal of All Subjects before the Subject Removal Date

When all the condition precedents have been met and you are ready to remove subjects, set up a time to meet with your agent who will draw up a separate addendum stating that you are removing all the subjects at the given subject-removal time or earlier. After you have signed it, the addendum is sent to the seller and the seller's agent. At this time, your agent will need to obtain the deposit from you in the form of a bank draft equal to at least 5 percent of the total purchase price. This amount will go into a trust account of the real estate agency.

Note that even if you are an experienced buyer or have a legal or real estate background and know about contract law, it is still a good idea to have a legal representative to assist you in all real estate transactions.

## The Deposit

The agent or legal representative who drafts your offer can draw up an addendum stating how and when the deposit funds will be placed into trust.

Both parties must agree to the new terms and must sign the addendum. You may make the down payment in instalments, but only if the seller agrees.

## What if the deposit cheque is NSF?

If a buyer's cheque is returned NSF, the seller must be informed of the situation right away. If the seller agrees, the buyer may be given a short period in which to provide a certified cheque, bank draft, or money order. If, however, the money is not replaced, the seller must be fully advised of the situation to obtain legal advice. The buyer must also seek legal advice.

## Where does the deposit go?

Your agent will have written in the contract of purchase and sale that the deposit goes into an interest-bearing trust account and that the interest on the deposit will be given to you at completion. Typically, only lawyers, notaries, and real estate agencies have trust accounts.

Never pay cash when you are paying for your deposit. A bank draft or certified cheque must be made out to the real estate agency "in trust," so that there is no mistaking where the deposit will go. If the seller turns out not to be the registered owner of the property, having the cheque deposited into a trust account will ensure that the money is protected.

# Checklist 2
# SUBJECT REMOVAL

Your offer has been accepted and now your job is to remove the subject clauses within a specified period of time. The following checklist will help you through the subject removal process:

❏ Have both you and the seller set out a time limit for the removal of subjects? Specify:

_____

❏ What are the subjects you have listed? _____

_____

❏ Have you secured a building inspector?

❏ Have you read the building inspector's report?

❏ Have you read the documents that were provided to you by the agent? Check documents that are applicable to your situation:

**Strata Unit**

❏ Form "B" or estoppel certificate

❏ Registered strata plan, amendments, and resolutions dealing with changes to the common property

❏ Current bylaws and last two years' minutes

❏ Financial statements

❏ Engineer's report or building envelope report

❏ Title search

❏ Property condition disclosure statement (Strata Title Properties Act)

**Single-Detached Family Dwelling**

❏ Property condition disclosure statement

❏ Title search

❏ Survey certificate

❏ Building inspection report

❏ Have you secured your mortgage?

❏ Have you verified the size of the dwelling, and are the room measurements approximate?

❏ Have you signed the Addendum stating that you will remove the subjects?

❏ Have you provided a bank draft or certified cheque made out to your real estate agency "in trust"?

# Chapter 13
# CLOSING COSTS FOR BUYERS

The completion date is the date on which you become the registered owner of the property. It occurs when you pay the purchase price in trust to the seller's notary or lawyer. "Closing" is a process in which all the legal and financial obligations in your contract of purchase and sale will be met.

Once the subjects written in the contract of purchase and sale have been removed and you have a legally firm contract of purchase and sale, you will need to retain a lawyer or notary to assist you with the closing procedure of your purchase. The lawyer or notary will start by perusing a title search on the property and will make the necessary inquiries regarding property taxes, maintenance fees (for condos), special levies, builder's liens, GST, commissions, deposits, and insurance to determine the exact amount owed by the buyers to the sellers on the completion date. If you are taking out a mortgage to finance your purchase, the lawyer or notary will also prepare the documents as instructed by the lender.

The lawyer will arrange an appointment with you so that you can review and sign all the relevant documents at his or her office. The documents will provide you with an overview of the total cost of this transaction (including adjustments, the property transfer tax, and the lawyer or notary's legal fees and disbursements) and balance owed to the seller on the scheduled completion date. This balance of funds needs to be made available to the lawyer or notary at least one business day before the completion date by way of a certified cheque or a bank draft payable to the lawyer or notary in trust. A statement of adjustments will be made that states the amount that has been credited or debited to your account.

## What Happens at Completion?

On the completion date, your lawyer or notary will submit the transfer document and your mortgage, if you have one, for registration with the provincial or territorial land title office. He or she will also forward your payment of the net purchase price to the vendor's lawyer or notary, and you will advise the real estate agency of the registration particulars, providing them with the authorization to deal with the deposit that is held in trust.

Once the registration of the purchase is complete, the purchaser's lawyer or notary will advise the seller's lawyer or notary that a cheque is available for pickup. Once the funds are received, the notary or lawyer will ensure that if monies are owed to the bank, the property tax department, the property management company, or any other party, they are paid before the net balance is made available to the seller.

Problems may surface during the closing procedure. For example, someone with the same name as you may have a court judgment against him or her, and the bank may refuse to release funds even though you sign an affidavit confirming that this person is not you. Or it may be discovered that the garage or pool of the property you are purchasing extends onto a neighbouring property, municipal setback, or utility right-of-way. You may be ordered to remove the encroaching structure. These occurrences may result in delays. To ensure that your transaction can close on time, you are advised to buy title insurance, which will allow you to take possession as scheduled, saving you any additional costs and inconvenience.

## Title insurance

Title insurance is something that few people know anything about until it's too late. It is a one-time premium paid to insure your right of ownership in real estate for as long as you have an interest in the property. It can insure for defects in title that might otherwise prevent a transaction from closing or that may arise after the property is purchased. It is now recognized and accepted by all major Canadian financial institutions. The cost of title insurance varies with the purchase price. In British Columbia,

Alberta, Saskatchewan, and Manitoba the price is $200 for transactions under $200,000. In the Yukon, the Northwest Territories, Nunavut, Ontario, Quebec, and the Atlantic provinces (New Brunswick, Nova Scotia, Prince Edward Island, Newfoundland and Labrador) the prices vary somewhat but are approximately $250 if the purchase prices are less than $200,000. There is a $50 additional policy for lenders.

The potential problems for which title insurance provides protection were discussed in Chapter 3 (see page 24).

The title insurance policy does not cover every situation. Here are the exceptions to coverage:

- Defects known to the recreational-home owner but not disclosed to the insurer before closing, or if the buyer agrees to accept the defects
- Defects that do not cause a loss to the recreational-home owner
- Environmental hazards
- Certain rights the government may have to the land
- Fair value of the home

Talk to your real estate agent, title insurance agent, or lawyer/notary who can inform you of all your options.

Two other valuable features offered by some title insurance companies are fixed closing costs and deferral of closing costs. A fixed closing cost is a fixed payment that buyers pay for their closing costs. Instead of allotting anywhere from 1.5 to 5 percent of the purchase price for closing costs, fixed closing costs allow buyers to budget more precisely.

Deferral of closing costs allows the buyer to defer the costs for registration, legal fees, and land transfer taxes for up to six months, with no interest charges. The buyer must pass a credit check and there is an administration fee of approximately $199. You can repay the open loan anytime before the six-month limit. After the six months, you will be charged 19 percent interest by Wells Fargo Bank.

## Fire and liability insurance

The mortgage lender will insist that you purchase a fire and liability insurance policy that guarantees that, in the event of a fire, the lender will receive the balance owing on the mortgage loan before you receive any insurance proceeds. This insurance must be in place before the completion date. You will be required to pay costs for fire insurance directly to the fire insurance agent.

Your legal representative will be required to provide written confirmation to the mortgage lender that fire insurance is in place and that the lender's interest under the mortgage has been noted on the policy of insurance. Costs for this written confirmation can vary.

## Additional Closing Costs

In addition to fire and liability insurance and title insurance, there are a variety of costs you may incur upon closing. Being aware of these costs will save you needless anxiety at completion. If you did not go with the fixed closing cost or the deferral of closing costs option when you purchased title insurance, closing costs amount to approximately 1.5 percent — and in some cases, up to 5 percent — of the purchase price. The following is a list of some of the costs you may incur, depending on your province or municipality.

## Adjustment costs

The adjustment date is the date on which the buyer becomes responsible for all bills related to the property, such as property taxes, utilities, and in the case of condominiums, maintenance charges, condo surcharges, and a fee for strata forms. The adjustment date and possession date in a contract are usually the same date.

If you purchase a recreational home and take possession on September 15, for example,

the sellers will have already paid the property taxes for the entire year. An adjustment will be made so that you pay the sellers the amount of property taxes due for the period September 15 to December 31.

Let's consider another scenario: you purchase and take possession at the end of the year, and the taxes for the year were long overdue but have not been paid by the seller. In this case, the taxes will be shown in the statement of adjustments and will be debited from the seller and taken from the proceeds of the sale.

## Utilities

Some municipalities do not include utilities such as garbage pickup and access to water and sewage systems in their annual tax bill. If that is the case, these services are usually billed annually, usually payable upon receipt. In some municipalities, utility bills are paid two, three, or four times a year. As with property taxes, you are responsible for paying from the closing date to the end of the year.

## Maintenance fees

If you are buying a strata-titled property (condo), you will probably have to pay maintenance fees to a strata corporation. These fees cover the cost of insurance, management fees, and the upkeep of the common property. They are payable to the strata corporation monthly, usually on the first day of each month.

## Condominium surcharges

Condominium surcharges apply in some provinces, territories, and cities. In Ontario, condominium surcharges are included in the closing costs, with a higher charge for high-rise units and a slightly lower charge for low-rise units. For example, some condominiums have "move-in fees" and "move-out fees" that apply when you move into a building, especially if the building is a new high-rise. Typically, fees of this sort will appear in the strata bylaws.

### Strata forms

Strata properties require certain forms to be filed at the land title office and with the relevant financial institution. These forms are usually provided by the management company and a small fee (approximately $15 to $35) is charged for them.

## Transaction levy

The transaction levy is unique to Ontario, where recreational-home buyers may be required to pay $53.50 ($50 plus GST) to the Lawyers Professional Indemnity Company on some title-insured transactions. There are some exclusions; you may want to contact your legal professional for more information.

## Appraisal fee

When the lending institution requires an appraisal of the property before approving your loan, it may be your responsibility to pay the appraiser's fee.

## Survey certificate

The lending institution may require a survey certificate. A survey formally establishes the boundaries of the property in a single-family dwelling, ensures that all buildings are within those boundaries, and ensures that your house is situated on your lot and is not encroaching on other properties. Typically, a survey is handed down as a courtesy from one property owner to the next. If the current owner cannot provide a recent survey certificate, or if there have been any recent upgrades or additions to the property (such as a deck or garage), a new survey certificate is required. However, a survey certificate is not usually necessary when you purchase title insurance.

## New home fees

Some provinces and territories levy additional fees for new homes. These fees are applied to the costs of new home warranties, education levies, tree planting, pavement grading, and installing water meters. The fees vary by province, territory, and municipality.

## Legal fees

The transfer of property ownership from seller to buyer must be recorded in the land title office to protect the new owner's interests. You will probably want to hire a lawyer or notary public who specializes in conveyancing to act on your behalf during the completion of your purchase. Your lawyer or notary public will charge a fee for this service, plus disbursements, including the land title registration fee. Disbursements typically include filing fees and title search fees. If you are financing your purchase with a new mortgage loan, there will be a further fee and disbursements to prepare and register the mortgage documents.

## Homeowner's insurance

Although only fire and liability insurance are mandatory (if you have a mortgage), you will likely want to consider more broad-based insurance for your recreational home. Most cottages can be insured with a homeowner policy; however, there are a few differences between cottage insurance and residential-home insurance. For example, burglary can be covered, but not theft. This means that the owner must prove there was forcible entry in order to file a claim. Also, the collapse of a roof due to the weight of accumulated snow may not be covered.

If you are leaving your property unattended for an extended period of time, or if you intend to rent out your property for either long-term or short-term periods, you should inform your insurance agent so that appropriate adjustments can be made to your insurance policy. Make sure you understand exactly what is and is not covered in your policy.

## How much will insurance cost?

A comprehensive policy will cost the most, but it will protect your recreational home's physical structure and contents on an all-risks basis. A named perils policy costs less but may not cover all the damages you could suffer. Home insurance deductibles can run anywhere from $200 to $10,000. The higher the deductible, the lower the premium.

Discounts may be available for recreational-home owners who have installed smoke alarms, sprinkler systems, or monitored burglar alarms. Some insurance companies also offer discounts to customers as a reward if they have had a long relationship with the insurance company, or if they purchase all their insurance (car, home, life) from the same company.

The larger the risk the property carries, the more expensive insurance will be. For example, if you purchase an older recreational home, or one with a wood stove or an underground oil tank, you may pay higher insurance premiums. Location is also a factor. Building a recreational home in a known flood zone may increase the cost of coverage, or you may not be able to get coverage for water damage. How many claims the previous owner of the property has made may also have an impact on the cost of insurance. If the recreational home has been broken into 15 times, you may find it quite expensive, or even impossible, to get coverage.

Be sure to consult an insurance agent about the policy that best suits your needs, and do so preferably as soon as you take possession.

# PART 3
## SELLING YOUR RECREATIONAL PROPERTY

Recreational Property for Sale!

For Sale by Owner!

SOLD

# Chapter 14

# WHAT IS YOUR RECREATIONAL HOME WORTH?

If you are thinking of selling a recreational home or property, there are many things to consider before a "For Sale" sign goes up. Whether you are planning to sell on your own or with an agent, it will take a lot of co-ordination, organization, and work. But usually the first thing that is on a seller's mind is how much the property is worth.

## Why Are You Selling?

One of the key questions that buyers will ask is your reason for selling, your motivation. Perhaps you or your spouse would like something bigger or smaller, or something in a different location. Maybe you have gone through a divorce and have to sell the vacation home as part of the divorce settlement. If you are selling for personal reasons that you do not want to disclose, talk to your agent about the best way to withhold personal information.

However, if your motivation has to do with the property itself — for example, if the condominium you own has a special assessment forthcoming, or your cottage needs major renovations that you don't want to do yourself — the guiding principle to remember is: any information that may negatively affect a buyer's decision to purchase must be made known to him or her.

## How Do You Know What Your Recreational Home Is Worth?

There are two basic ways to find out how much your recreational home is worth in today's market — in other words, its market value. You can engage a real estate agent to provide you with a Comparative Market Analysis (CMA), similar to what you received when you were purchasing, or you can hire an appraiser to help you determine the value of your home. Many agents will provide a CMA free of charge in the hope that they will establish a rapport with you and you will list with them or will refer them to friends or family. An appraiser will charge you for the service.

Agents determine what the recreational home is worth by looking at active, sold, and expired listings in the area and base their price on what the market is doing over a short period of time, say three months in an active market. Appraisers work for the banks and make their evaluation of what a recreational home is worth based on land values, the home's condition, etc. In general, appraisers tend to be on the conservative side when providing a value to a home, and it may differ from the purchase price that buyers are willing to pay at a given point in time. In short, the difference between an appraiser and an agent is that appraisers provide sellers with an estimate of what their recreational home is worth, while agents indicate what the market is willing to pay.

It is not a good idea to price your recreational property yourself without an appraiser or an agent to provide you with crucial data and information about market statistics. Many sellers, when they see that a neighbouring recreational home sold for a specific price, want that exact same price (or better) for their own. However, each recreational property is unique, and each property's value will depend on many factors such as the age of the home, the square footage, upgrades to the kitchen, bathroom, electrical and plumbing systems, and so on.

Although you can use the Internet to get an idea of the prices recreational homes in your area are selling for, it is always a good idea to ask a professional for help to get the best price.

## Comparative Market Analysis (CMA)

As discussed in Chapter 11, a Comparative Market Analysis (CMA) is a comparison of similar properties that have recently been sold. It operates on the principle of substitution, assuming that the market value of the subject property is

equivalent to prices recently paid for similar properties.

When the CMA is used for single-family dwellings, it compares the seller's property with others in the same neighbourhood of the same general age, square footage, lot size, number of bedrooms and bathrooms, amenities, frontage and depth, and so on. For condominiums, a comparison is made with active, sold, and expired listings in the same building or a similar building nearby. In other words, a condominium will not be compared to a single-detached home, as they are not in the same class.

An agent prepares a CMA report by collecting and analyzing market sales data for all of the similar properties sold in the previous six months to a year. He or she will also look at the market conditions and at active and expired listings within the same time frame to determine the best value of your recreational home.

## Pricing land only

If you are selling land only, without any improvements such as a cottage, chalet, or other building, you will be pricing it against other land-only properties in the area. It is important to note that some financial institutions will require a larger down payment for purchasing vacant land, and buyers may not always qualify for this type of financing.

## Increasing or Decreasing Your Price

If your recreational home has been on the market for a while and has not sold, or if you have not had any offers, you should consider changing the price you are asking. It may be that the market has changed and prices have dropped, or there may be more or better recreational homes for sale. You can obtain a more recent CMA and adjust the price to reflect the market. Most agents update their clients' CMAs on a regular basis to make sure they are in touch with the market and have priced their homes accordingly.

It is not uncommon for sellers to increase or decrease their prices. They could make a change for a number of reasons:

- If the price was more than or less than fair market value to begin with.

- If the market has changed from a buyer's to a seller's market or vice versa. For example, if it has become a buyer's market and there are a lot of properties on the market, you might want to decrease your price so your property is more attractive to buyers. If it is a seller's market, with few properties competing with yours, you may want to increase your price.

- If you have already placed an offer on another property, you may want to sell faster to avoid having to apply for bridge financing.

- If it is a "soft" market, without too much activity, as often happens during the fall and winter, you may want to lower the price.

If you list your property on the MLS system, buyers are aware of the listing date, so they know if a property has been on the market for a long time. If it has been, they may assume there is a problem with the property and will avoid it or make an offer below the asking price. Buyers also have the sales history available to them, so they know if the price has increased or decreased. If it has decreased, they will want to know if there is a problem with the property or if the seller's circumstances have changed — for example, if the seller has already purchased another recreational property.

Likewise, if the price has gone up, they want to know why it was increased. It is always a good idea to price your home at fair market value from the start, so buyers don't get suspicious. To avoid this problem, most agents would just cancel the listing and re-list the property again with a new price.

If you are working with an agent and you decide you want to reduce your price, you must give the agent authorization in writing, even if you have discussed a price reduction orally. Everything that pertains to real estate must be done in writing.

If you are selling your recreational home on your own, without an agent, you should be aware that most sellers of FSBOs price their homes according to what they would like the property to sell for, rather than what the market is willing to pay. Be careful you don't fall into this trap. Have your recreational home professionally appraised and ask a realistic price for it.

# Chapter 15
# GATHERING DATA AND LEGAL DOCUMENTATION

When you are preparing to sell your recreational home, it is important to gather pertinent information before you put it on the market. You may need to order some of the legal documents ahead of time, but if these documents are valid for a limited time, such as a Form "B" or financial statements, you may want to hold off ordering them until your property has an accepted offer.

Other documents may already be in your possession, and it is simply a matter of searching for them and gathering them together. It's a good idea to stay ahead of the game by making the documents readily available for potential buyers should they ask to review them before or after placing an offer. The following are the main pieces of information and documents you will need:

- Title search
- Mortgage information (the title search will show if there is an outstanding mortgage or clear title to the property)

- Survey certificate (if one is available)
- New-home warranty information
- Property condition disclosure statement
- Oil tank removal invoice, certification, documentation, and photos (if applicable)
- Invoices for work done recently (e.g., renovations, repairs, etc.)
- Warranties (for newer appliances and renovations)
- Zoning information
- Municipal assessment (for property taxes)
- Recent utility bills

If you are selling a strata title property, you will need the following additional documents:

- Form "B" or estoppel certificate
- Minutes from strata meetings and AGMs
- Strata plan
- Bylaws and house rules

- Amendments to the bylaws
- Co-op shares
- Engineer's report
- Financial statements
- Maintenance fee information
- Zoning information

Checklist 3 at the end of this chapter will help you keep track of the documents you have gathered.

# Title Search

A title search will let you and potential buyers know who is registered as the current owner of the property. It will also indicate if any registered mortgages, restrictive covenants, easements, or rights-of-way may affect the use or value of the property in either a positive or negative way.

It is important to do a title search to ensure that you, as a seller, are able to convey title to the buyers on the completion date. If the buyer suffers a loss because you cannot convey title, you (and your agent, if one is involved) can be held liable.

The other reason to do a title search is to ensure "genuine consent" on the part of the buyers. This means that the buyers understand what they are buying and are aware of everything that could affect their title if they buy the property. It is important that the legal interest being sold is either free of any charges or that these charges are disclosed. There might be financial charges, such as mortgages or a builder's lien, a certificate of pending litigation, or physical encumbrances such as easements or rights-of-way.

If you are using a real estate agent, you can ask him or her how to read the title search. Otherwise, you may want to consult a lawyer. You should know that most title search information is very basic. It will show that there is a charge against the property, for example, but will not show the details of the terms, interest payments, and so on.

# Survey Certificate

A survey formally establishes the boundaries of the property, ensures that all buildings are within those boundaries, and ensures that your recreational home is not encroaching on other properties. A survey certificate is often handed down as a courtesy from one property owner to the next, so you may well have received one when you purchased your home. However, if you have made recent upgrades or additions (such as a deck or garage), you may need to get a new survey certificate. Not all buyers require such a certificate, so don't have a new survey done unless it is requested.

# Property Condition Disclosure Statement (PCDS)

Regulatory bodies and real estate boards throughout North America have introduced property condition disclosure statement (PCDS) forms to address concerns about health, safety, and environmental protection in relation to homes (see Sample 3 on page 68). Regulators have set stringent levels for safety, greater disclosure, and broader responsibilities and liabilities in relation to these matters. Buyers, sellers, and current and former owners, as well as the seller's agent, share in that responsibility of potential liability.

The intent of a PCDS from a seller's perspective is to document the history of the property and its current condition in writing. It is signed by the seller and dated. It provides the seller with written proof that the deficiencies or defects were disclosed to the buyer and that the buyer knew of these deficiencies.

In past decades, asbestos insulation and urea formaldehyde foam insulation (UFFI) have attracted interest as possible health risks. Recently, the presence of radon gas, lead pipes, and even lead-based paint found on older properties has been a concern to buyers. These issues are covered on the PCDS forms.

If you know about a problem and do not reveal it to a buyer, or if you misrepresent a property by falsifying documents, this is very serious as the buyer can sue you under the common laws of agency, contract, and negligence. If you are not aware of a problem, then you may not be entirely liable. If you are in doubt, seek the advice of legal counsel immediately.

Many provinces and municipalities have their own property condition disclosure statement forms, as areas of concern may vary from one area to another. You can obtain a PCDS form that addresses issues pertinent to your area from your local real estate board.

Buyers are expected to do their own due diligence to find out whether the property they are purchasing is a high risk or not. The purchase of any recreational home has some risk, and it is up to buyers to look at these risks and figure out whether they are comfortable with them. They should confirm the statements in a PCDS by, for example, inquiring about renovations or improvements and ascertaining when they were done. If you state that the roof shingles were replaced two years ago, buyers may check the date by asking to look at the invoice or by contacting the roofer. Some building inspectors read PCDSs and take the time to verify or deny what has been written.

If you are unwilling to fill out a property condition disclosure statement, many buyers may simply walk away from your property. They may assume you are hiding something. Others will hire a qualified inspector to perform a full inspection of the property. If you are using a real estate agent, he or she may not be able to post the listing on the local real estate board's Multiple Listing Service. Some boards and associations have made completion of a PCDS mandatory for every real estate listing.

# Oil Tank Removal

Many underground heating-oil tanks have reached the end of their useful lives and are beginning to corrode, rust, and leak. If you have had an oil tank removed, this should be mentioned in your property condition disclosure statement. This is a positive feature, as most buyers would prefer this problem to have been dealt with; if an oil tank has not been removed, buyers might ask for the purchase price to be reduced.

If you have had an oil tank removed, potential buyers need to know when this work was done and the name of the oil tank removal company. They will likely want to see the following documents:

- A copy of the oil tank removal certificate.
- Photographs documenting the removal.
- A report from the oil tank company stating that there were no signs of oil contamination.
- A certificate from the fire department stating that the soil in the surrounding area was not contaminated.

You should check with your municipality about local codes and regulations regarding oil tanks. A real estate agent can also help you with this and can provide a list of contact names and numbers for companies in your area that remove oil tanks.

# Zoning Information

Local governments designate zones for certain areas to specify the types of buildings that may be built on particular properties and how those buildings may be used. For example, there could be single-family or multi-family residential, duplex, commercial, or industrial structures. Look for zoning information on your title and include this in the information that you provide to potential buyers.

## Municipal Assessment

Buyers will want to know how much you have been paying for property taxes, as this may influence whether they can afford to purchase your recreational property. If you do not have the current year's tax bill available, contact the municipal assessment office for a copy.

## Restrictions

If you are selling a strata title property or a recreational home in a new development, you must inform potential buyers of any restrictions on the property. Go through the strata corporation bylaws, rules, regulations, and amendments to find restrictions or prohibitions imposed on an owner's ability to rent or use the property. Restrictions are not necessarily a negative issue for recreational-home buyers. For example, restrictions that limit or prohibit rentals may be a positive factor for buyers. The fact that the people living in a building own their units generally has a positive impact on upkeep.

## Other information for strata property

The Form "B" or estoppel certificate, issued by the property management company, indicates how much money is in the contingency or reserve fund.

Minutes from strata council meetings document issues and business dealings that have come up in relation to the property. For example, they may cover discussions about maintenance and repair programs for the upkeep of a building.

Bylaws specify how a condominium establishes its house rules and restrictions. Bylaws are made, amended, or repealed by the board of directors. They are not effective unless the owners of the majority of units vote in favour.

If the home you are selling is part of a co-operative, you will be transferring co-op shares rather than land. You should have a copy of your share certificate, which indicates how many shares you hold, as well as any particulars concerning the rights that are for sale, such as the suite location and other exclusive areas.

An engineer's report, prepared by a professional engineering company, will give details of the structure of the building, the building envelope, and the foundation of the building. Some reports will include recommendations on work that should be done and price estimates.

Financial statements indicate revenue (funds generated from monthly maintenance fees) and expenses (such as maintenance costs and management costs). They are prepared by the condominium corporation for each fiscal period.

Maintenance fees paid by owners of condos, townhouses, and detached houses in developments cover the costs of insurance, management, and upkeep of common property. In some instances they may also include the cost of gas and hot water and/or yearly taxes. It is important that you list details of these maintenance fees in any information you hand out to potential buyers. If you are not sure what is included in maintenance fees for your strata property, call your property management company for details.

## Other Documentation

If recent renovations or new appliances are selling points for your property, you should have invoices available so buyers can see exactly when work was done or when appliances were purchased. You should also have copies of any warranties still in force for renovations or appliances. Recent utility bills will indicate how much a buyer should expect to pay for electricity, heating, etc. If you have copies of maintenance records for equipment included in the purchase, such as a gas fireplace, furnace, sprinkler system, hot water tank, or air conditioner, you may want to make these available to the buyer as well.

# Measuring Your Property

It is important that you know the measurements of your recreational home and property, as many buyers will ask for the dimensions of the home and of each room so that they can determine whether it will satisfy their needs. You can do the measuring yourself, but if you are in doubt about how or what to measure, you can opt to hire a professional measurement company to measure your recreational home. Contact your real estate agent for names of professional measurement companies.

If you are doing the measuring yourself, be aware that you measure only the total finished area of the building. In residential buildings, do not include porches, decks, and patios (whether they are closed in, screened in, or open); garages or carports; crawl spaces and areas underneath dormers, or other unfinished areas situated below grade (underground). These areas should be listed separately on your information sheet under a description of the property. Include the warning "Buyers to verify their own measurements" in all literature you hand out so that buyers will perform their own due diligence by verifying measurements.

If you are selling a condo, you should not include balconies, large patios, or parking stalls in the condominium measurements. Instead, look at your strata plan for information. It is best to define the condominium by reference to the walls of the buildings. Developers, in an attempt to increase the apparent size of a condominium unit, have often included outside areas, such as balconies and large patios, in their measurements, but these are in fact part of the common property, with each unit owner having exclusive use of the area adjacent to his or her unit.

When you advertise your condo, you should indicate the square area of the condominium, together with any exclusive-use areas, as in the following example: "This condominium is 1,212 ft$^2$, together with exclusive use of patio, large balcony, and one parking space." This defines what is being offered and eliminates confusion about the measurement of condominiums.

# Pre-Sale Building Inspection

Until recently, when properties went on the market, the common practice was that a buyer made an offer "subject to approving and being satisfied with a building inspection." After the inspection, sometimes the seller suddenly learned about various problems that he or she may not have known about. To avoid such surprises, more and more sellers are opting to have a pre-sale home inspection done before they list their property. This is an out-of-pocket expense for the seller, but it is worth the cost for the peace of mind it gives you. Such an inspection will identify problems you may not know about, but which would show up in a buyer's inspection. If you know of these problems ahead of time, you can either adjust the price accordingly or fix the problems before the house goes on the market.

Arranging for a pre-sale inspection not only helps you determine a fair market price for your recreational home, but also shows buyers that you are being upfront, fair, and honest in representing your property.

## Checklist 3
# DOCUMENTS AND INFORMATION

**The following are the main pieces of information and documents you will need:**

❏ Title search

❏ Mortgage information (the title search will show if there is an outstanding mortgage or clear title to property)

❏ Survey certificate (if one is available)

❏ New-home warranty information

❏ Property condition disclosure statement

❏ Oil tank (if applicable):

    ❏ removal invoice

    ❏ certification

    ❏ documentation

    ❏ photos

❏ Invoices for work done recently:

    ❏ renovations_____

    ❏ repairs_____

    ❏ maintenance report_____

❏ Warranties:

    ❏ appliances_____

    ❏ renovations_____

    ❏ other _____

❏ Zoning information

❏ Municipal assessment

❏ Recent utility bills:

    ❏ hydro

    ❏ electric

    ❏ cable

    ❏ telephone

    ❏ other _____

    ❏ other _____

## Checklist 3 — Continued

**You will need the following documents if you are selling a strata title property:**

❑ Title search

❑ Mortgage information (the title search will show if there is an outstanding mortgage or clear title to property)

❑ New-home warranty (for new condos)

❑ Property condition disclosure statement

❑ Warranties:

    ❑ appliances_____

    ❑ renovations_____

    ❑ other _____

❑ Form "B" or estoppel certificate

❑ Minutes from strata meetings and AGM

❑ Strata plan

❑ Bylaws and house rules

❑ Amendments to house rules and bylaws

❑ Co-op shares

❑ Engineer's report

❑ Financial statements

❑ Maintenance fee information

❑ Zoning information

❑ Municipal assessment

❑ Recent utility bills:

    ❑ hydro

    ❑ electric

    ❑ cable

    ❑ telephone

    ❑ other _____

    ❑ other _____

# Chapter 16
# SELLING ON YOUR OWN OR WITH A REAL ESTATE AGENT

After gathering data about your recreational home, you should now decide if you are going to sell your recreational home on your own, or if you are going to engage a partial-service or full-service real estate company. You should consider the following factors when making this decision:

- Cost of selling the recreational home
- Your personality and ability to do the job
- Pitfalls of selling without a real estate agent
- Services offered by agents

## What Are the Costs of Selling a Recreational Home?

As a seller, there are a variety of costs that you will incur whether you sell your recreational home on your own or with an agent:

- Appraisal to determine your selling price

- Land title search
- Recreational home inspector's fee for a pre-sale inspection
- Hiring a professional measurement company
- Marketing (e.g., print ads, flyers, website, signage, distribution of print materials)
- Lawyer's or notary's fees to draw up the final paperwork
- Cost of paying off your mortgage before the agreed-on term ends

If you are selling your recreational home on your own, all these costs will be immediate out-of-pocket expenses. If you are engaging the services of an agent, most of them will be covered by your agent and deducted from his or her commission after your recreational home has been sold.

# Do You Have What It Takes to Sell Your Own Recreational Home?

Many people have the "do-it-yourself" gene. They want to do as much as they can themselves without having to hire anyone, least of all a professional.

If you are one of these people, you should assess your personality and skills before deciding to sell your own recreational home. You may want to ask yourself the following questions:

- Are you able to communicate effectively with potential buyers who have serious questions about your property?

- Can you accept feedback about your property, either positive or negative, without taking it personally?

- Will you be able to differentiate between bogus customers and bona fide buyers who are ready, willing, and able to purchase?

- Do you have the tenacity and perseverance it takes to sell a property?

- Are you outgoing and gregarious, or are you shy and easily intimidated?

- Can you adapt to a variety of different situations?

- Do you know enough contract law and real estate law to be aware of your legal responsibilities to the buyer so that you will minimize risks and potential liabilities and lawsuits?

In assessing your own personality, you need to admit your limits. If you realize you need help for some aspects of the sale, or if you are overwhelmed with the tasks that need to be done, hire someone to lend a hand or give you advice (e.g., a tax accountant, a real estate agent, a lawyer, etc.). Professionals are trained to perform a number of tasks and may have many years of experience that allow them to foresee problems that could arise. They know what extra steps to take to ensure that delays do not occur.

They can usually put you in touch with other professionals who can give you help or advice in other areas of selling your recreational home.

If you tend to be an introvert, buyers could misinterpret your body language and get the feeling that you are "weird" or untrustworthy. This is a major drawback for selling on your own, as it is crucial that buyers trust the seller and feel at ease with him or her. There have been several recent cases of tenants, or even people with no connection to a property, posing as the seller and persuading buyers to pay out thousands of dollars in deposit monies (sometimes cash). As a result, buyers tend to be on their guard and may not consider buying a recreational home if they feel uncomfortable with the seller.

Even if you decide that you don't have the ability to sell your recreational home on your own, there are many aspects of selling that most people can do, such as arranging viewings and hosting buyers at showings or open houses. If you decide that you can sell your recreational home on your own, the legal aspects of real estate should always be dealt with by a lawyer.

# What Are the Pitfalls of Selling without an Agent?

If you want to sell your recreational home on your own, you should be aware of the advantages and disadvantages of being a seller of a FSBO, and the public's perception of FSBOs.

The advantages are that you don't have to pay the real estate agent's commission, which can be a substantial saving, and you have the satisfaction of accomplishing a difficult task on your own terms.

Sellers of FSBOs often tend to price according to what they would like their recreational homes to sell for, rather than what the market is willing to pay. If you are selling your recreational home on your own, make sure potential buyers know that you have priced your property according to fair market value. You may want to show them comparable listings in the area.

Buyers who view FSBOS may be looking for a bargain and will try to get you to lower your price, arguing that you don't have to pay commission so you shouldn't be asking so much.

Real estate agents are subject to a code of ethics and are bound by Canadian laws to ensure a seller fully discloses a property's condition. As a result, if a seller does not engage an agent, buyers may question whether the seller is fully and honestly disclosing health and safety risks, water damage, moisture ingress, and other problems. When buyers' agents see a property is a FSBO, they may shy away from it, believing it's too big a risk because the seller may not disclose the history and problems of the property, or what is disclosed may be inaccurate.

One way to get around the reluctance of buyers' agents when you are selling your recreational home on your own is to work with the agents and pay their commission in the event they produce a qualified, willing buyer to place an offer on your property. You would have to negotiate the fee with the buyer's agent and should take into account the following factors:

- The price that the buyer is willing to pay for your recreational home

- The number of offers or requests for viewings you have had (i.e., if you've had no activity, you'll be more motivated to pay a commission)

- Your capital gain if, for example, you purchased the property at a low price and are now selling at a high price

- Your margins if you have not spent much on marketing

Often you will pay approximately half the regular commission, which is what the buyer's agent would get if your property were in an MLS listing. Other times, if the buyer's agent has had to do more than the usual work because you

were late producing documents or didn't understand the legal complexities and the buyer's agent had to explain everything, he or she may want a full commission.

# What Are the Benefits of Selling with an Agent?

Agents have knowledge of the process and the market, so they are likely to get the best possible price for a property. They have a lot of experience dealing with people and situations and can act as a negotiator or mediator, bringing both parties to a mutual agreement. They can deal with the myriad marketing, legal, financial, and organizational details — helping you as much or as little as you want. They can identify potential problems and help you avoid them, or they can deal with the problem before it becomes a major issue. And if things do go wrong, you can go to the real estate agency or the industry association to get satisfaction.

Agents also perform many duties "behind the scenes" that are not always apparent to the seller. They answer buyer and agent questions about the property or the seller, verify information the seller has provided, arrange appointments to view the recreational home, and after showing it will try to get some feedback, either from the buyers who view the property or their agents, about what they thought of the property, its condition, price, and so on. This information may help you make a better decision on price points.

## Choosing the right selling agent for your recreational property

If you decide to go with an agent to sell your home, it is important to choose the right agent for you. You should go through an interview process so that you will know exactly what services each agent provides and what type of marketing tools he or she uses to sell property.

It is also important to look at the agent's credentials, referrals, and testimonials, as well as to find out if the agent you are considering has ever faced a disciplinary hearing or if any complaint has been made against him or her. To get this information, you can call the real estate council of the province or territory in which the agent is licensed. The council provides licences and training for real estate agents.

There are many ways to find an agent. Referral is one good source. Ask friends, family, neighbours, and colleagues who have recently sold a recreational home if they would recommend their agent. You can also study print ads or websites, including www.realtor.com and www.mls.ca, which allow you to identify agents based on their location and specialties.

For some sellers, using a well-known name is important. Some buyers buy based on an agent's name or reputation. Many agents who have been in the industry for a long time have carved out a niche for themselves, specializing in a geographic area or demographic type. If you are selling a property suitable for such an agent's demographic or geographical specialty, you should consider using that agent. Other agents have a reputation for service and customer satisfaction. Perhaps there is an agent you or your family has worked with in the past. If you feel comfortable and familiar with that name, buyers might too.

Equally important to some people is branding and company name recognition. The Canadian Real Estate Association (CREA) defines "branding" as the proprietary visual, emotional, and cultural image that you associate with a company or product. When you think of Volvo, for example, you might think of safety. The fact that you remember the brand name and have positive associations with that brand makes your product selection easier and enhances the value and satisfaction you get from the product. The same thing works for real estate agencies — you have a better feeling about some over others because of personal experience, stories you've heard

from friends and colleagues, or even company advertising you've seen.

If you have a sense that buyers are drawn to a certain agent or agency due to personal or company name recognition, you might consider talking to that agent or agency about selling your property.

## Agents specializing in rural land

Selling farmland or hobby farms requires an agent with a specialized background. If you have acreage for sale, you should choose an agent who is familiar with official plans, zoning bylaws, types of agricultural uses, and so on.

# Types of Listings

There are three basic types of real estate listings in Canadian markets: open, exclusive, and Multiple Listing Service (MLS).

## Open listing

This is a relatively loose verbal agreement in which the seller gives one or more than one real estate agency the authority to find a buyer for the property.

## Exclusive listing

An exclusive listing gives one agent or agency the authority to offer a property for sale, lease, or exchange during a specific time period. The seller agrees to pay the listing agent a commission, even if the seller eventually sells the property himself or herself.

## Multiple Listing Service

A Multiple Listing Service (MLS) is an exclusive listing with an added marketing feature. This service is operated by local real estate boards; for example, a property in rural Nova Scotia might be listed by the Annapolis Valley Real Estate Board. When you sign a multiple listing form, you authorize your agent to co-operate with other agents who are members of the real estate board.

Your property will be listed on MLS, reaching thousands of agents, and posted on the websites www.mls.ca and www.realtylink.org, reaching the general public as well. This enables people to view your listing 24 hours a day, seven days a week, including photographs of your property and all pertinent information. You can even include a virtual tour of your property, with several pictures or videos allowing for 360-degree views of each room.

The MLS feature sheet is an important document because potential buyers rely on the accuracy of the information. An MLS feature sheet contains an in-depth description of your property, as outlined in Chapter 1.

The MLS system provides information about your property to other boards in other cities, regions, and countries. If you think about the number of investors and potential recreational-home buyers who might be thinking of moving to your area from other provinces or territories and even other countries, it becomes clear that the MLS system is a great marketing tool.

Agents also have access to regularly updated catalogues of MLS listings, which they can show to clients who do not have Internet access. This catalogue, however, which is produced monthly, may be outdated.

# The Listing Agreement

The relationship between a seller and a listing agent is outlined in a contract called a listing agreement, which ensures that both you and your agent have a complete understanding of your rights and responsibilities. You will each know what you can expect and what is expected from each other.

The listing agreement legally defines your arrangement with the agent and sets out in writing the following terms and conditions:

- The price you are asking for your property and your terms of the sale.
- The existing financing arrangements and whether the financing can be assumed by the new owner.
- A list of items that are attached to the building (the "fixtures") that are not to be included in the sale. For example, light fixtures, fireplace inserts, and so on are typically part of the sale price, so if there is a fireplace insert or crystal chandelier that you don't want to part with, you need to specify this. To avoid confusion or misunderstanding, you may want to take photographs of fixtures that are not to be included in the purchase price.
- The dates on which the contract begins and ends.
- The date a new owner can take possession.
- The commission the agent will receive once your home is sold.

Before you sign a listing agreement, ensure that everything has been filled in properly, and that you understand all the terms in the contract. An example of a listing agreement is provided in Sample 4.

Your agent should provide you with a copy of this agreement. Keep that copy in a safe, accessible place for future reference. The listing agreement is a legal contract. You cannot simply terminate it without the consent of your agent. If your agent says that you can cancel the listing agreement at any time, ensure that you get this in writing.

# Responsibilities of Listing Agents

Once you have listed your property for sale, the listing agent has a legal duty to protect and promote your best interest at all times. He or she owes you — the principal — his or her undivided loyalty and must disclose to you all information

## Sample 4
# LISTING AGREEMENT

**LISTING AGREEMENT**

Name of owner(s)/seller                          Listing agent

BETWEEN: _____  AND  _____

_____                          _____

Address/Telephone number                          Address/Telephone number

_____                          _____

_____                          _____

1.  **Listing authority and term:**

    The Seller hereby lists exclusively with the Listing Agent the property described until
    11:59 p.m. on _____/_____/_____
                         month       day      year

2.  **Property:**

    _____                          _____
    Unit no.                          Address of property

    _____                          _____
    City/Town/Municipality                          Postal Code

    Legal description:_____

    _____

    PID: _____

3.  **Terms of sale:**

    _____                          _____
    Listing price                          Terms

4.  **Listing agent's remuneration:**

    _____

    _____

**5.    Co-operating agent's remuneration:**

_____

_____

SIGNED, SEALED AND DELIVERED THIS _____ DAY OF _____ , 20 ____.

_____
Seller's signature

_____
Witness to seller's signature

_____
Seller's signature

_____
Witness to seller's signature

_____
Listing agent (print)

_____
Per: salesperson's signature

_____
Salesperson(s) (print)

obtained from any source that might influence your decision. The listing agent should not reveal to another person any confidential information that might jeopardize your bargaining position. She or he has a duty to exercise due care when answering questions and to treat all parties fairly and honestly.

The legal and professional requirements for agents are outlined in Chapter 3; please refer to pages 17 to 21. Most listing agents are members of the Canadian Real Estate Association (CREA). CREA members are governed by a professional code of ethics and standards of business practice. They are required to meet financial and educational standards and to demonstrate integrity and character necessary to protect the public. Members support free and open competition, which means they decide for themselves the commission rates or fees they charge for services offered to the public, the division of those fees among co-operating members, and whether they work full time or part time, as part of an agency, or on their own. The code of ethics encourages creative but honest advertising, and discourages members from filing complaints against competitors based on competition-related issues such as fee structure, comparative but truthful advertising, or acceptance of open or exclusive listings.

## The agent's commission

Agents work on a commission basis and receive payment only after the successful completion of a sale. The commission is usually stated as a percentage of the total sale price or as a fixed dollar amount. GST is charged on a commission.

The commission rate is not fixed by law or by any real estate board, and it varies throughout Canada. It must be negotiated between you and the agent you engage to help you. The commission rate often reflects the quality and quantity of service an agent provides. It is important that you, as a seller, do your due diligence and find out what type of service best suits you.

You should thoroughly discuss the commission before you sign a listing agreement. You and your agent should decide on the amount of compensation, the sources of payment, and the time or occasion on which the payment is to be made. All these details should be included in your listing agreement.

The listing agent traditionally shares his or her commission/fee with the agent working for the buyer. In the case of an MLS sale, your agent might also pay other brokers, agents, and salespeople who helped bring in a buyer. (The portion of commission shared in this instance is called a "commission split" and is often spelled out in the MLS listing.)

## Chapter 17
# MARKETING YOUR RECREATIONAL HOME

After gathering the data about your recreational home, deciding on a listing price, and deciding on a marketing budget, your agent — or you, if you're selling on your own — will prepare a marketing plan, along with brochures or flyers, advertising, a website, a feature sheet, and a schedule of open houses.

## What Do You Do to Market a Property?

Once you have determined the selling points of your recreational home and the target market, you need to set up a marketing plan. There are a variety of methods for letting people know your recreational home is for sale, and you can use some or all of the following methods:

- MLS listing (unless you are selling a FSBO)
- Classified ads in newspapers or real estate papers
- Display ads in newspapers or real estate papers

- Flyers to be delivered in a targeted neighbourhood or posted where your target market will see it
- Information sheets that are distributed to prospective buyers visiting the recreational home
- Website with pictures, floor plans, and other information about the recreational home
- Open houses

## Print advertising and websites

If you are a seller of a FSBO and doing print advertising (classified or display ads), take some time to look at similar ads that are already running. This will give you an idea of what information you should include and how you should set up your ad. If you are including a picture in a display ad, make sure that it is a good quality photo and will reproduce well in the newspaper. You may need to hire a designer to put the ad together. The same goes for flyers and information sheets. You want to present a professional image to potential buyers. Unless you have website production skills, you should probably hire an experienced web designer if you want to advertise your property on the Internet.

If you are selling on your own, you will pay for marketing up front and will either spend time producing ads and a website or will pay for someone to do it. Though you may not want to spend money on advertising, such expenditures are a crucial part of the home-selling process unless you can arrange a private sale by word of mouth.

If you hire a real estate agent, he or she will incur some of these costs as part of a marketing plan and will deduct the costs from the commission after your property is sold. Ask your agent to itemize exactly which costs are included and which are not. The type and amount of advertising an agent does depend on the state of the real estate market at the time you are selling. Some agents spend up to 25 percent of their commission on marketing and "farm advertising," in which print advertising featuring your home (e.g., flyers, mail-outs, newsletters, and Just Listed cards) is sent out to a specific neighbourhood.

Most agents today also produce an Internet marketing plan to showcase and market your property around the world. Someone relocating from the United States, Asia, or Europe, for example, can view your property online from the comfort of his or her home. This may include a virtual tour of your property.

## Signage and tools of the trade

If you are selling your home on your own, you will incur costs to purchase "tools of the trade." An example is For Sale signs with your phone number. If your property is not in a busy area, you may want to put up directional arrows to show where the recreational home is located. You could put up balloons, flags, colourful banners, or similar paraphernalia to draw attention to your property, just as agents do when they are advertising an open house.

There may be restrictions on the type, number, and/or placement of signs, so check your community's zoning bylaws for a provision limiting the use of outdoor and indoor advertisements and other graphic displays. Many municipalities throughout Canada have instituted restrictions regarding For Sale and Open House signs. For example, some municipalities restrict the use of directional signs at main intersections as they are a distraction — especially in high traffic areas or where signs may restrict visibility. Even rural municipalities have restrictions about the size and number of signs, so it is a good idea to do some research before investing in signage.

Other tools of the trade you might want to invest in are a cellphone, a digital camera, and business cards with contact numbers.

## Marketing to friends, relatives, and neighbours

Be sure you let friends, relatives, and neighbours know you intend to sell. In the case of condominiums, tenants or homeowners in the building may have friends or relatives who want to purchase a unit in the same development.

If you end up selling privately, with no real estate agent involved, it is a good idea for both you and the buyer to obtain legal representation to draw up the contract of purchase and the final bill of sale, and to ensure that the title is clear.

## Advertising

Whether you are creating print ads, classified ads, brochures, and a website for a FSBO or to reduce the commission you pay an agent, here are some marketing dos and don'ts to remember:

- Newspaper advertising should be brief but to the point. Remember that each line of print costs you money, so use it well. Price and location are important, as are the number of bedrooms and bathrooms, and, if you have room, the square footage of living area and lot size for detached houses.

- Don't include the street address in your advertisement, just a phone number to call. This will prevent people coming by at all hours to view the property. Sellers of FSBOs need to be sure that people viewing their recreational home are serious about buying, so it's a good precaution to try to get a sense of a person over the phone, judging his or her manner, attitude, questions, and so on. Not including your address in the ad will also protect you from potential robbers.

- Indicate any restrictions, such as no pets or no rentals, in order to eliminate some calls.

- Be creative in your advertisement, but don't embellish. Use descriptive words that will target your market — "private patio" or "low maintenance." Always use action words, such as, "Call today!" "Don't delay!" "Make an appointment!" "Be the first to see it!" Action words help potential buyers feel emotionally involved. Avoid words that may be offensive or childish.

- Make sure that your telephone numbers are correct. You should include work numbers and cellphone numbers if you have them; real estate is a 24/7 job, and buyers or their agents need information right away. If they have to leave a message on voice mail or with an answering service, they may not wait for the answer. (Don't forget, if you have to be away from home or work, to forward calls to whoever is helping you sell your recreational home.)

- A picture is worth a thousand words. For brochures or feature sheets, make sure that you have a clear photo of the front of your recreational home. Avoid taking photos at night or on a cloudy, rainy day. Equally important are multi-photo "tours" of your recreational home that include shots of the interior and exterior. If you have a waterfront, lake, or city view, be sure to show it to potential buyers. (For security reasons, do not leave out precious items, family heirlooms, jewellery, artwork, and so on, when you take photos. Thieves sometimes check out photos of houses on sale to see if there is anything worth stealing.)

- When describing your home, use words and features that are enticing. An example of a brochure or website text would be:

  *Fabulous southern exposure on Six Mile Lake with breathtaking views. Immaculate 2 bdrm cottage with 210 ft of pristine rock and pine tree shoreline. Small beach and deep water that is excellent for swimming. Pine floors and floor-to-ceiling stone chimney with airtight wood stove. Newly renovated kitchen has large island and handmade rustic pine cupboards. 90% winterized, modern septic system, small cabin/storage shed at water's edge. Plenty of room to expand or to build a new cottage.*

- Be honest in your print advertising. Exaggerations and misrepresentations will not only result in lost sales, but will lead you into trouble. If, for example, you say in your ad, "Unit has 5 appliances," but then you decide you don't want to sell the appliances, the buyer can go back to the ad to prove that the appliances are part of the purchase price and must stay with the unit. Don't describe a home as "solid," when it is actually a tear-down, or claim a property has hardwood floors when they are just plywood or laminate. Don't include "water view" as a feature in your listing if you have to stand on tiptoes and crane your neck to catch a glimpse of the water!

- For agents, misleading advertising reflects poorly on the industry. If it violates CREA's code of ethics and standards of business practice, the agent may face discipline by his or her board or association. Misleading advertising is also a criminal offence, and agents or individuals who produce misleading ads can be sued by the buyer on the grounds of misrepresentation. The general prohibition against misleading advertising applies to both the literal wording and the general impression created by an advertisement in determining whether the ad is misleading in a material respect.

Recreational Property for Sale!

For Sale by Owner!

SOLD Realty 213-555

# Chapter 18
# SHOWING YOUR RECREATIONAL HOME

Statistics tell us that 95 percent of buyers purchase based on emotion. Buyers need to absolutely *love* your recreational home if they are going to purchase it. To capture the attention of buyers, some agents hire an interior designer to help prepare a recreational home so that it achieves its maximum selling potential. Often designers will move, or remove, furniture to highlight certain features or functionality.

## Showing Made Simple

Some agents use home stagers or set designers to prepare high-end recreational homes for show. Home staging companies offer services that range from simply organizing the home so it is free of clutter and adding touches such as dramatic lighting, luxurious throw pillows on a sofa, and abstract paintings on the walls, to removing all the furniture and storing it for a few days and replacing it with rented furniture. The aim is always to earn a higher price and faster sale.

Your real estate agent can recommend a home stager in your area, or check the Yellow Pages or on the Internet.

When developers or real estate agents are selling a new development, they will involve architects, designers, and interior decorators to make the most of their show homes and demonstrate the latest in light fixtures, colour, and design trends. These homes can give you ideas and inspiration on how to show your recreational home.

## Providing access to a recreational home

If you are selling a vacation home that is far from your primary residence, you should consider all your options for selling the property in the most efficient way (and avoiding the time and money involved in commuting back and forth to the property). You may want to consider the following options:

- You can provide keys to the potential buyer if you are not worried about giving a stranger access to the property. In this situation, you need to assess the risk to you and decide if the person is a bona fide buyer. In addition, you may want to discuss this option with your insurance agent.

- Alternatively, you can provide keys to the potential buyer after obtaining a security deposit — perhaps a credit card number, a certified cheque, or a deposit of some amount.

- You could leave your keys with a trusted friend or neighbour who lives near the property and who is willing to show the recreational home to potential buyers.

- You may want to hire a real estate agent in the area to sell your home. Most agents do not go out of their specific geographical area but are very knowledgeable about their own locale, so obtaining an agent in the area can be the best way to sell a vacation property.

# Open Houses and Agent Tours

As part of your marketing strategy, you should host a public open house to showcase your recreational home to potential buyers and to agents. If you are using a real estate agent, he or she will likely arrange an open house specifically for agents during the first week the recreational home is listed. This event will be on a weekday, and all agents who are members of the local real estate board will be invited. Buyers may also attend if they are available, but most buyers attend open houses on weekends.

If you are selling your recreational home on your own, it is difficult to let all the local agents know about your open house in a cost-effective way. Even using your time to e-mail agents in your area about the open house may not be fruitful. The best option may be to contact the top ten agents in your area to see if they have any clients who may be interested.

It is important to know the dos and don'ts of showing your recreational home to potential buyers and agents. The following are some tips for showing your home, either at an open house or for a private viewing:

## Dos

1. Do be professional at all times. Greet each person who comes in, and wear appropriate attire. You want to look professional but also approachable, so good-quality casual clothes are okay, but not sweats, shorts, or grubby T-shirts.

2. Do ask visitors to sign a guest book so that you will know who has attended.

3. Do make sure that you have all the data in your feature sheet correct. Buyers rely on the accuracy of the information provided, such as the total square footage, size and measurements of the living area, and so on.

4. Do make sure that you have plenty of feature sheets to hand out.

5. Do have the lights on. Even if it is daytime, leave the lights on so that people can see everything.

6. Do ask a friend, relative, or neighbour to open the door for buyers and agents should you be late for an open house. Do not be late for a private showing — make sure that you leave ample time to get to your house and prepare it for viewing. Most buyers' agents have tours scheduled and show homes one after the other. If you are late, chances are the buyers will not wait and will move on to the next home.

7. Do make the beds, tidy up the insides of closets, clean bathrooms, and remove all garbage. You could also turn on the fireplace, turn on the music, and light some candles for ambience.

8. Do provide a contact name and number where you can be reached at any time of the day and night and on weekends.

9. Do put a sign out for your open house before and during the event. Signage is an important tool in the real estate industry. Place a sign at your recreational home and directional signs on the main streets or roads. Attach balloons, flags, and other attention-grabbing items to your recreational home and the sign in front of it.

10. Do bake muffins! Studies have shown that the smell of goods baking in the oven stimulates the senses and gives the feeling of being "at home."

11. Do ask agents to leave their business cards behind. It is always important to find out who has come into your home, and you may want to take the opportunity, especially if you are selling your recreational home on your own, to call the agents back to find out if their clients liked the recreational home and if they could provide any feedback about the recreational home — for example, if it is priced fairly.

12. Do have open houses on weekends and at times when there are other open houses in your area. Usually this is afternoons between 1 p.m. and 3 p.m. during the fall and winter, and from 2 p.m. to 4 p.m. during spring and summer.

13. Do open your storage lockers, sheds, and basements to show potential buyers all the storage area that is available to them.

14. Do make sure that you provide buyers and their agents with room to park. If parking is too difficult, buyers may get frustrated and move on to the next property. Instead, provide buyers with directional signs indicating where to park.

# Don'ts

1. Don't have a showing during or around mealtime. Some foods may be fragrant to some, yet offensive to others.

2. Don't be around if you have a hard time accepting negative comments about your taste in décor (or lack thereof). If you are selling with an agent, you can have him or her host the open house. If it is a FSBO, ask a trusted friend or relative to be the host.

3. Don't have young children or elderly people at the recreational home during a showing. Potential buyers want to feel free to move about the recreational home without intruding on other people's spaces.

4. Don't be misleading about something important to the buyers. If you don't know the answer, ask them to leave their name and phone number so you can get in touch with them after you find the answer to their question.

5. Don't be shy. If buyers come into your open house with food, or they come smoking cigarettes or wearing muddy shoes, ask them politely to remove their shoes or refrain from eating or smoking until after they leave.

6. Don't have pets around — barking dogs can scare potential buyers away, and cats may set off allergies. Have someone take your pets away while you are showing your recreational home, or leave your dog in its kennel.

7. Don't be alone! Make sure that you have friends or family members working alongside you. This way you can make the most of an open house. If you are showing a cottage, for example, you may want to show a group of buyers the full lot and the beach access across the street, at the same time as other people are viewing the cottage. If you are showing a condominium, the strata corporation may insist, for the safety and security of other homeowners, that you escort all visitors and guests in and out of the building. You would need more than one person helping you to do this.

8. Don't sit down! Make sure that at all times you are busy showing guests around the property — after all, open houses don't last very long!

9. Don't turn your back on these strangers or let them browse through the rooms on their own. If you notice suspicious behaviour, whatever it is, pay attention to your gut feeling. If you feel very uncomfortable, there is nothing to prevent your refusing someone to enter your home.

10. Don't leave out sharp objects — knives on the counter, for instance — or anything else that could be of harm. Make your recreational home as safe as possible.

11. Don't leave valuables — jewellery, cash, keys, artwork, coin and stamp collections, or anything that can be carried away quickly — lying around your home. Some thieves pose as buyers and are really there to steal from you. Ask people with knapsacks to leave their bags in the front foyer.

12. Don't have an all-day open house. Have the recreational home open for two or three hours during the time when the general public is out looking.

## Protecting Yourself

When dealing with the public, you need to be careful not to put yourself in harm's way. You are vulnerable at open houses and even more so when meeting a complete stranger for an appointment to view an isolated, vacant recreational property. Agents often double up when they are hosting an open house or showing a property, and this is good advice for FSBOS as well. Have a friend or your spouse accompany you. Make sure that someone knows of your whereabouts at all times. Carry a cellphone with preset emergency numbers, establish a distress code with family members, and do not include the word "vacant" in your advertisement.

## Chapter 19
# THE OFFER

As you show your recreational home to people at an open house or privately, the buyer's body language will give you a hint whether he or she likes your property or not. One of the telltale signs of approval is a buyer smiling and nodding while you are talking about the features of the home. Another sign is a buyer asking a lot of questions about the property. It means the buyer is trying to obtain as much information as possible about the recreational home so that in the event he or she makes an offer, it is based on facts rather than just emotion.

If you see buyers with their cameras out, you will know that they are interested in your property — generally only those who are seriously interested take pictures. Buyers who take their time going over the property, carefully examining bedrooms, bathrooms, and kitchen space, are also sending a signal that they are interested in your property — especially when they envision their furniture in the home. Statements such as,

"This could be the guest room," or "Our big dining room table will go perfectly here," suggest that the buyers are interested.

Finally, buyers who request a second or third showing or buyers who physically measure room sizes, especially when they bring along a friend or family member, are definitely interested in the property. Often buyers have already made up their mind, but they need a second opinion to help them in their decision-making process by pointing out possible problems they have overlooked or by confirming their positive feelings.

## Separating Qualified Buyers from the Lookers

As a seller, you will also want assurances that your interests are protected and that potential buyers are capable of paying what they offer for your property. Especially if you are selling your recreational home on your own, it is difficult to distinguish qualified, willing buyers from people who are just curious neighbours. Some buyers say that they have financing in place even when they don't.

Most buyers' agents today will prescreen their clients to determine their capacity before taking them out on tours to view properties. Buyer qualification is the process of uncovering a buyer's motivation, needs, desires, and ability to pay, although it is not an exact method of determining a client's capacity or ability to obtain financing. Some buyers' agents will ask all potential clients for a copy of a letter of commitment from the buyer's financial institution. This will show exactly how much mortgage financing the person is pre-qualified for and how much purchasing power they have. It will also show the agent that the client has taken the time to go through the pre-qualification process. If you are selling on your own, you can ask a potential buyer for a letter of commitment to ensure he or she can obtain the financing for a recreational home purchase.

# Who Can Be Legally Bound to a Contract?

It is important to note that to be legally bound to a contract, the parties entering into the agreement must be legally competent. Infants or minors, mentally incapacitated persons, and intoxicated persons are protected by law so that others will not take advantage of them. The age of majority differs in each province. In Alberta, Saskatchewan, Manitoba, Ontario, Quebec, and Prince Edward Island, the age of majority is 18. In British Columbia, New Brunswick, Nova Scotia, Newfoundland and Labrador, Nunavut, the Northwest Territories, and the Yukon, it is 19.

# When You Receive an Offer

In real estate, everything must be in writing, so if someone verbally offers to buy your recreational home, you don't actually have an offer until the buyer has written it down in a contract of purchase and sale.

When you, as a seller, receive an offer from a buyer, there are several things you should look at to evaluate the validity of the offer. These include the condition precedents or subject clauses (including time clauses and financing clauses), the buyer's letter of commitment, and the amount of deposit being offered.

## Condition precedents

As was discussed in Chapter 12, on any offer presented to you, there will be condition precedents or subject clauses. These outline conditions that must be met before the buyer agrees to finalize the purchase. If you skipped reading Chapters 11 and 12, now is a good time to read those chapters to review what goes into an offer and how subjects are removed.

When going through an offer, if you are uncertain about any of the condition precedents, seek legal advice immediately. If you accept the offer and sign it, you have accepted the terms and conditions in the contract.

## Multiple offers

In a seller's market, or if your property is unique or priced well, it is not uncommon to receive more than one offer. When you have two or more offers for your property, look carefully at the price, terms, conditions, financing, and, in particular, dates of completion and possession set out in each offer. Sellers of FSBOs should contact a lawyer or the law association of their province or territory to find out what rules apply for accepting multiple offers. Make sure that you understand how each offer comes into effect, especially if you accept one offer and then accept another offer as a backup. If there is a real estate agent involved, fully discuss the agency's policies regarding multiple offers and the sequencing of offer presentations.

No two offers are identical. They may be identical in price, but there will be other terms and conditions that make each buyer's situation unique. If you can, meet with the buyers. You can probably get a good sense of their financial capabilities by asking for their financial information up front, before accepting their offer.

You can choose one buyer over the other according to your personal preference. Perhaps you want to see your recreational home sold to a family rather than a developer, or vice versa. Maybe you're in a hurry to sell, and one buyer offers an earlier completion and possession date.

## Lowball offers

If you are selling your recreational home on your own, don't be surprised when you receive lowball offers. Many buyers, when they see a property is a FSBO, tend to make an offer well below the seller's asking price, thinking that it may be accepted. But there can be lowball offers for properties that aren't FSBOs as well.

Sometimes, buyers' agents will ask you or your agent why you are selling. If the buyer's agent believes you are highly motivated to sell, he or she might think that a lower offer will be accepted. If you are dealing with an agent and are not motivated to sell unless you get full price, you should tell your agent to clearly state that the seller wants only full price. Otherwise, it is a waste of everyone's time to have offers presented for less than the full price. If you are selling on your own, you can state in ads and information sheets that the price is firm and there will be no negotiation on price.

## Negotiating a Sale

When you receive an offer from a buyer, you have three choices. You can —

- accept everything exactly as written,
- reject the offer altogether, or
- counter the offer.

If you accept the offer as it is written, you have a legally binding contract to sell your recreational home. If you reject the offer or make a counter-offer, you are entering into negotiation, because if you reject an offer, the buyer or the buyer's agent could ask you why you rejected it and make a new offer.

When you counter an offer, there is usually a time limit during which the counter-offer is valid. Time is of the essence and both parties have a legal time limit to respond to offers and counter-offers. Once that time has expired, there is no offer in place. It is important for a seller to be available by phone, cellphone, or pager after he or she has made a counter-offer. The seller's agent must be able to contact the seller with information of a buyer's counter-offer. You should be available to receive the call and respond quickly.

Negotiating is a process that takes time, effort, understanding, and patience. For some people, this process is an art form that is perfected with experience. For others, negotiation is a stressful and difficult process, especially when it involves a real estate transaction. Many times, emotions take over. Lack of communication or jumping to conclusions can also lead to problems. For example, a seller may be insulted by a lowball offer, when in fact the buyers have made an offer based on their financial capabilities.

Face-to-face negotiations with a third party — a real estate agent, lawyer, or other unbiased but knowledgeable person — are recommended to help you and the buyer achieve your goals. Remember that negotiation calls for compromise on both sides. Both parties have to listen and communicate effectively, and when it comes to real estate, this communication must be clearly set out in writing. Changes to the contract are not binding until they have been written down and initialed by both parties. Verbal offers and counter-offers can be rescinded at any time. (If there is so much crossing out and initialling on the contract that it becomes difficult to read, either party can draw up a new contract. Make sure that it contains all the terms and conditions that you have already agreed on.)

Promises or guarantees made by the seller outside the normal transaction, and outside the written contract of purchase and sale or agreement to purchase, must be written in an addendum that is signed and dated by both parties. Both the seller and the buyer should have a copy of the addendum so that there is no mistaking the legal responsibilities of both parties. If either the seller or the buyer, or both, are using a lawyer or notary public, these people should also have copies of the addendum.

## What to negotiate

Sellers often negotiate for a higher price than the buyer has offered, but there are other equally important items to negotiate, including the following:

- Condition precedents
- Condition precedents removal date
- Fixtures and chattels: Fixtures are items that stay with the property and are usually attached by a nail, screw, or something similar (i.e., light fixtures, wall-to-wall carpet). In addition, there may be items that are not apparent to the buyer; for example, a storage locker in a strata title property or an outdoor gas lamp for a cottage. A description of these should be included in the written contract or addendum. A chattel is an item that is not part of the property, and can therefore be removed by the seller.

  Anything that is a fixture but is not for sale should be stated in your feature sheet and noted as an exclusion in the disclosure statement. A buyer may want to include items that you have excluded from the property for sale. You need to decide if you will agree to sell these and if

you will negotiate to increase the sale price as a result.

- Closing and possession dates
- Down payment or deposit (After condition precedents have been removed, the deposit is usually increased to at least 5 percent of the sale price.)

## Selling your furniture

If you want to sell your furniture, this should be a separate transaction altogether and should not be included as part of the negotiations or purchase price. Deal with the contract of purchase and sale first, without any mention of the furniture, and afterwards, let the buyers know that you are also interested in selling the furniture for an additional cost. Including this in the contract of purchase and sale could cause problems or complications with the offer.

Have a list that names each piece of furniture (include a digital photo so that there is no mistaking which coffee table you are referring to) and give this list to the buyers. If they are not interested in the furniture, this will not collapse the deal, as this issue was not included in the main body of the contract of purchase and sale.

## When You Reach an Agreement

After you reach an agreement with a buyer, you still have to wait for all condition precedents to be removed before the sale is final. Many things can happen that could result in a sale not going through. For example, the buyer may not be able to get financing, the building inspection could reveal that major repairs are needed, or the buyer may feel there is not enough money in the contingency fund for a strata title property. If problems arise — as they sometimes do — seek legal counsel immediately and make sure that the buyer signs a release form or an addendum to indicate that he or she was unable to remove condition precedents.

In some circumstances, *you* may suddenly change your mind about selling. Many sellers feel seller's remorse, especially when an offer and acceptance of an offer happen quickly, as they usually do. You may be able to rescind the offer while you are still negotiating by simply refusing to accept one of the buyer's changes, but you should talk to a lawyer first to obtain proper guidance. If both you and the buyer have signed the contract of purchase and sale, including all changes, and the condition precedents have been removed, you cannot back out of the contract unless you can prove in a court of law that you were not legally competent to enter into a contract to begin with.

## What if the recreational home does not pass inspection?

There are three facets to a recreational-home inspection:

1.  To cite problems that need to be addressed immediately.

2.  To cite problems that will need to be addressed in the near future.

3.  To provide maintenance programs.

If the recreational home fails an inspection, there are three likely scenarios:

1.  The buyer walks away from his or her offer.

2.  The buyer will renegotiate the price to reflect the amount of repairs that need to be done.

3.  If the buyer agrees, the seller may do the repairs and not renegotiate the price. This may be tricky, as the buyer may want a guarantee of the work being done to a certain standard.

The art of negotiation comes into effect once again, as this is a volatile situation in which anything can happen. As a seller, you need to decide whether you would like the deal to collapse or if you want to renegotiate at this point. It is always

a good idea to consult with the home inspector (even though his or her client is the buyer) or to see a copy of the report so that you can make a decision based on information from a qualified professional.

## Showing after Accepting an Offer

Once you have accepted an offer and are preparing to negotiate, you should still show your property to other potential buyers in case the first offer collapses. As you can see, there are many things that still need to happen, even after an offer is in place. It is always a good idea to show while there is still an interest in the property.

## When Condition Precedents Are Met

After the conditions are removed, you need to make sure that the buyer has drawn up a new addendum that says the conditions have been removed and that the buyer and witnesses have signed this addendum. Also make sure anything that was changed or amended in the contract of purchase and sale is duly initialled or signed and is dated properly. All parties should have a copy of the contract to keep for their files.

Ensure that the down payment cheque has been deposited in trust at your lawyer's or real estate agent's office and that all pertinent documents have been sent to your conveyancer — the lawyer or notary who completes the transfer and register of title (the conveyancing) to the new owner.

Checklist 4 at the end of this chater provides questions to ask yourself as you draw up a contract.

## Suspicious Transactions

When selling your property, especially if you are selling a FSBO, you should be aware of suspicious transactions. The federal Proceeds of Crime (Money Laundering) and Terrorist Financing

Act (PCMLTFA) was created in 2000 to deal with criminal activities such as money laundering and the financing of terrorist activities.

There may be any number of things about a transaction that seem okay at first glance, but altogether should raise alarm bells. Be suspicious of the following:

- The buyer offers to pay for the recreational home with a significant amount of cash.
- The buyer places the property in the name of another person other than a spouse.
- The buyer's name is different on the offers to purchase, closing documents, and deposit receipts.
- The buyer negotiates a purchase for market value or above asking price, but records a lower value on documents and pays you the difference under the table.
- The buyer pays a substantial down payment in cash and the balance is financed by an unusual source, such as by an offshore bank.

If you feel you are dealing with a suspicious transaction, log on to the Financial Transactions and Reports Analysis Centre of Canada's (FINTRAC) website at www.fintrac.gc.ca for more information, or seek legal counsel immediately to find out what appropriate steps you should take.

# Checklist 4
# THE CONTRACT

**The following checklist will help remind you of the details to consider before you sign the contract:**

❑ What offer was placed on your property? $ _____

❑ Did you receive a counter-offer?

❑ If so, are you going to accept, reject, or make another counter-offer? (This process of counter-offers may continue until an agreement is reached.)

❑ Did you include a time and day in which your counter-offer will expire?

❑ Were legible copies of the contract provided to all parties?

❑ Were changes in the contract initialled by all parties?

❑ Were signatures obtained by all parties?

❑ Were signatures of witnesses obtained by all parties?

❑ When is the subject removal date? _____

❑ When is the inspection date? _____

❑ What down payment and/or deposit was made? $ _____

❑ Is the deposit going to be paid in full or in stages?_____

❑ What is the completion date? _____

❑ What date does possession take place? _____

❑ Are there other dates you would like to negotiate? Specify: _____
_____

❑ Do you know what the price includes and doesn't include?

❑ Did the price include storage space? (If so, what number? _____)

❑ Did the price include parking stall(s)? (If so, what number(s)? _____)

❑ Are there items the buyer would like to negotiate that were not included in the purchase price (e.g., light fixtures, alarm system)? Specify:_____
_____

❑ Have all the subjects been removed from the contract? (For example, subject to a building inspection, financing, review of the property condition disclosure statement, bylaws, minutes, etc.)

❑ If attachments or schedules form part of the contract, are these referenced in the main contract?

❑ Is the contract drafted to your specifications and particular situation?

## Checklist 4 — Continued

❑   Did you give a receipt to the buyer for the deposit and was it attached to the contract?

❑   If you have an agent, is he or she keeping the lines of communication open between you and the buyer during the negotiations?

❑   Did you, as a seller, include your own subject conditions in the contract?

❑   Did you, as a seller, communicate these subject conditions in writing as part of the contract?

❑   Now that an agreement has been reached, did you or your agent make sure the contract has been initialled, signed, and duly witnessed to ensure it is a legally binding contract?

## Chapter 20
# CLOSING, COMPLETION DATE, AND POSSESSION

The completion date is the date on which the buyer becomes the registered owner of the property. It occurs when the buyer pays the purchase price in trust to the seller's lawyer or notary. Closing is the process during which all the legal and financial obligations in your contract of purchase and sale will be met. Your agent, lawyer, or notary should keep you informed of the steps involved. The possession date is the day the buyer can move in.

## The Closing Procedure

Once the condition precedents written in the contract of purchase and sale have been removed and you have a legally firm contract, the buyer will go through the closing procedure. He or she will retain a lawyer or notary to make the necessary inquiries regarding the property taxes, builder's liens, GST, commissions, deposit, and so on to determine the exact amount the buyer owes you on the completion date.

The lawyer will arrange an appointment at which the buyer can review and sign all the relevant documents. The documentation provides an overview of the total cost of this transaction (including adjustments — i.e., fees for utilities, property taxes, insurance, etc., that the new owner owes for the balance of the year — and the property transfer tax and the lawyer's or notary's legal fees and disbursements) and indicates how much money (if any) the buyer still owes to complete the purchase on the scheduled completion date. The buyer must make this balance of funds available to the lawyer or notary at least one business day before the completion date. Usually it is paid by way of a certified cheque or bank draft payable to the lawyer or notary in trust.

While this is happening, you need to make sure that everything is in order, especially with regards to your title to your recreational property. If there is a lien on the property or a certificate of pending litigation, you will not be able to complete the sale. If you don't learn about an impediment until the completion date, and possession occurs on the very next day, there will be problems and the buyer may sue you for damages. An agent or lawyer should notice these issues well before closing and can deal with them in time. However, if you are selling a FSBO and have engaged a lawyer only to handle the transaction at the very last minute, it is up to you to be aware of any charges on your title.

If there are co-owners on the title, they must all sign the contract of purchase and sale in order for the sale to be legitimate. If the co-owners are out of the province or territory or out of the country, you must have a power of attorney from them that allows you to act on their behalf. Talk to a lawyer about obtaining a valid power of attorney.

# What Happens at Completion?

On the completion date, your lawyer or notary will submit the transfer document (which transfers title to the property from you to the buyer) to the land title office. Once the registration of the purchase is complete and the funds are received from the buyer, you will meet with your lawyer or notary to finalize documents. He or she will give you a statement of adjustments indicating in detail what you still owe. The notary or lawyer will ensure that if you owe monies to the bank, the agent, the property tax department, the property management company or strata corporation, or anyone else, they are paid before the net balance is made available to you.

There may also be money owing to you in the form of credits for property tax or strata fees paid in advance.

## Reimbursement of property taxes

If you have already paid the full year's property taxes to the municipality, the buyer will have to reimburse you for the portion of the taxes from the adjustment date set out in the contract of purchase and sale.

If you have outstanding taxes, either from the current year or previous years, a portion of the money from the sale of the property will be used to pay for the taxes. The seller must provide the buyer clear title, which means it must be free of all encumbrances such as liens, certificate of pending litigation, mortgages, and current property taxes. Your lawyer or notary will finalize papers and should attend to this before completion.

## Capital gains tax

Capital gains tax is a tax that a seller pays when selling a property, as set out in the federal Income Tax Act. While a capital gain arising from the sale of an individual's principal residence is most often exempt from taxation, the capital gain arising from the sale of a second property — for example, a vacation home — is taxable under this act. Secondary homes can include everything from cottages to timeshares, so expert advice from a tax accountant is highly recommended.

## Completion must be done on a weekday

Make sure that the completion date is not on a weekend or statutory holiday, as the land title office is closed at such times. If by some oversight the completion date does fall on a statutory holiday or a weekend, you should arrange to see your lawyer or notary at least a day or two before — when the land title office is open — so that there will not be any complications or delays. And if the buyer's lawyer is not able to register the buyer as the new owner of the property, then the seller can choose not to provide the keys until this has been done.

For this reason, it is always a good idea to make the possession day a couple of days after the completion day. This helps in the situation described above, and it is also a good idea because as a seller you want to make sure that the monies are transferred successfully and are in your account before you provide the buyers with the keys to the recreational home. If there is any delay in obtaining paperwork, you don't want to be in a position where you have to decide whether or not to hand over the keys.

If you have not previously read Chapter 13, turn to pages 81 to 83 and read the section What Happens at Completion. Along with describing some potential delays that could arise before the sale is finalized, this section also introduces title insurance, which can save both buyers and sellers additional costs and inconvenience.

# Possession

The possession day is agreed to by both the buyer and the seller. It is important to note that possession typically occurs at 12:01 p.m. on the possession day and not a moment sooner. This means that you are legally responsible for anything that happens before that time. However, if you indicated a different time in the contract of purchase and sale, either later or earlier, then that time on the contract is what both parties must adhere to.

## When do you hand over the keys?

It is important to provide keys to the buyer only at the exact time of possession — and only after you have received news from your lawyer or notary that the monies have been received and the title has been exchanged. Make sure that you protect yourself, especially at the last minute!

Even if you are selling a rental property and you know that the tenants have already moved out, you should not provide the keys to the buyers any sooner than the possession day. The buyers may ask you to give them the keys earlier so they can repaint or make repairs, but you are still the registered owner of the property and, as such, are still liable should anything happen that causes damage or injury.

## What should you leave behind on possession day?

On possession day, you should leave everything mentioned in the contract that is included in the purchase price. That means all fixtures should remain — things that are affixed to the walls, floors, or ceilings. That includes all window coverings, light fixtures, and so on, unless they were specifically excluded in the contract of purchase and sale.

As a seller, you should leave everything that the buyers viewed — you cannot substitute any of the appliances, window coverings, or fixtures with replacements of a lesser value or quality. Buyers and buyers' agents are thorough and take photos for documentation to ensure that appliances are the same type, model, and colour as when they viewed them.

## What should you not leave behind?

You should make sure that old, worn-out furniture, tattered area rugs, garbage, and anything else deemed part of the seller's chattels is completely removed from the premises. If the property has been rented to tenants, you should do a walk-through of the entire property to make sure that they have completely removed their belongings and have not taken anything that is not theirs to take away.

Though typically all fixtures are included in the purchase price of the home, you may have excluded certain specific items, either in the listing agreement with the real estate agent or in the addendum to the contract of purchase and sale. You should make sure these items are removed.

## Doing a walk-through with the buyer or buyer's agent

It is common practice for listing agents to walk through the property with their seller clients before releasing the keys to the buyer. This will ensure that everything is as it should be. Likewise, the buyer's agent will do a walk-through with the buyer to make sure that everything that was written in the contract has been left behind.

If you do not have an agent, you should do a walk-through yourself to make sure that the buyers are satisfied. Some misunderstandings could still occur at this time. Perhaps the buyers thought that the area rug was to be left behind, especially as it fit so nicely in the room. You will have to explain to them that it is considered a chattel and is not included in the purchase price. Another situation may be that former tenants may have left a locker full of items. Make sure, in the case of a condominium, that the parking spot and storage lockers are empty.

## A special touch

When you are leaving a recreational home, it is always nice if you take the extra time to vacuum the rugs, remove the garbage, and leave the place as clean and tidy as possible. Provide keys, remote controls for garage doors, and any pertinent information such as warranties and manuals for the new homeowners. Many sellers also leave a welcome card and perhaps some flowers for the new owners.

## Appendix
# COTTAGE ASSOCIATIONS OF CANADA

## National

**Cottager**

www.cottager.org

The Cottager promotes the interests of Canadian cottage owners and associations. If you cannot find a cottage association in your area, you may want to contact the Cottager for more information about cottage associations; they may be able to help you locate an association near you.

## British Columbia

**Floating Home Association Pacific/Canada**

www.floathomepacific.com

This site provides valuable information about everything concerning floating homes and marinas. Even if you don't have a floating home in the Pacific region, you may still find answers to questions you may have about this type of lifestyle.

## Alberta

**Association of Summer Villages of Alberta (ASVA)**

The ASVA provides leadership in advocating local government interests to the provincial government and other organizations, and provides services that address the needs of its membership.

## Saskatchewan

**Provincial Association of Resort Communities (PARC)**

www.parcs-sk.com

PARC is organized to promote the interest of resort communities in Saskatchewan.

## Manitoba

### Manitoba Association of Cottage Owners
http://maco.clickusfirst.com

This is an umbrella association of cottage, beach, and ratepayers' groups in Manitoba. It is an incorporated, non-profit association run by volunteers. Its goal is to promote and advance the common interest of ratepayers in cottage areas in Manitoba.

## Ontario

### Federation of Ontario Cottagers Association (FOCA)
www.foca.on.ca

FOCA is a non-profit, voluntary organization representing more than 500 Ontario cottagers' associations plus individual and corporate members. FOCA offers members information on a wide range of cottage-related issues including everything from taxation to water quality.

### Baptiste Lake Association
www.baptistelake.org

This Bancroft-area cottager association was formed in 1949. It provides newsletters and other vital information for its members.

### Gloucester Pool Cottagers Association (GPCA)
www.gloucesterpool.ca

The GPCA is the voice of its members regarding political, social, and environmental concerns. The GPCA website contains information on local history and events, and explores environmental issues of concern for cottagers as well.

### Lake of Bays Association
www.loba.ca

The purpose of this association is to promote, maintain, and enhance a clean, healthy, and natural environment, a well-serviced community, and a safe, peaceful Lake of Bays.

### Lake of the Woods District Property Owners Association Inc.
www.lowdpoa.com

The organization provides members with representation, assistance, and leadership with many cottage-related issues.

### Rondeau Cottagers' Association
www.rondeaucottagers.ca

The mission of this association is to protect, preserve, and promote the natural and historical environment of the Rondeau Park community.

### Temagami Lakes Association
www.tla-temagami.org

This cottage association is dedicated to ensuring that the "Tenets for Temagami," adopted in 1994, are embedded in all planning documents for the Temagami area.

# Watershed Protection Organizations

### Veins of Life Watershed Society
www.volws.bc.ca

A community-operated environmental organization based in Southern Vancouver Island that aims to establish a healthy and sustainable environment in which watersheds support fish and wildlife, and recreational use.

### BC Watershed Stewardship Alliance
www.bcwsa.ca

With 26 watershed regions currently operating throughout BC and the Yukon, BCWSA is a non-profit society representing grassroots community-based watershed organizations in these areas.

### North Saskatchewan Watershed Alliance
www.nswa.ab.ca

If you are living in northern Alberta along the Saskatchewan River, you may want to understand more about water quality. The North Saskatchewan Watershed Alliance encourages community-based stewardship in the North Saskatchewan River Basin.

### Partners for the Saskatchewan River Basin
www.saskriverbasin.ca

This organization promotes watershed sustainability through awareness, linkages, and stewardship.

### Muskoka Lakes Association
www.mla.on.ca

The Muskoka Lakes Association was established in 1894 to represent the interests of lakeshore residents in preserving the unique beauty of Muskoka. They promote the responsible use, enjoyment, and conservation of the Muskoka environment.

### Big Rideau Lake Association (BRLA)
www.brla.on.ca

BRLA is a non-profit organization with roots back to 1911. Located on the Big and Lower Rideau Lakes in Eastern Ontario, the association is committed to long-term environmental protection and service to all who use the lake and share its resources.

# GLOSSARY

**Addendum:** An addition to an offer in which changes made in the offer are noted.

**Adjustments:** The money the seller receives back for utility fees, property taxes, insurance fees, etc. that he or she has already paid for the year.

**Agent:** A person who assists in the buying or selling of real estate.

**Agreement to purchase:** See *contract of purchase and sale*.

**Appraiser:** A person employed by a bank who will give an evaluation of what a home is worth based on land values, the home's condition, etc.

**Assumable mortgage:** A mortgage that allows buyers to assume the mortgage from the seller instead of from a lending institution.

**Back-up offer:** An offer that, once it has been accepted by the seller, sits in secondary position and waits until the first offer firms up or collapses.

**Blanket mortgage:** A blanket mortgage is a type of mortgage registered over two or more properties. In the event of default, the lender could proceed against one or both of the properties in order to get sufficient proceeds from the sale to satisfy the outstanding debt.

**Bridge financing:** A temporary loan that makes it possible for a seller to purchase a new home when that sale closes before the sale of his or her current home.

**Building inspector:** An expert who thoroughly inspects buildings and provides a written report of defects that need to be addressed.

**Buy-down:** Money provided to a lender by a third party on a borrower's behalf to result in a reduced interest rate.

**Canada Mortgage and Housing Corporation (CMHC) Market Analysis Centre:** A service provided by CMHC that assists buyers and sellers in understanding the current housing market.

**Chapter:** A type of co-ownership similar to fractional and quarter ownership in which a chapter owner owns a property with nine other owners.

**Chattel:** An item that is not considered part of the property and that can be removed by the seller.

**Closed mortgage:** A mortgage contract that is written for terms ranging from six months to ten years. Penalties may be triggered if the borrower wishes to end the contract before the term expires (early repayment).

**Closing:** The process during which all the legal and financial obligations in a contract of purchase and sale are met.

**Commission:** The fee a real estate agent receives for selling a house. It is usually stated as a percentage of the total sale price or as a fixed dollar amount.

**Comparative market analysis (CMA):** A collection and analysis of market sales data for similar properties that have recently been sold. It assumes that the market value of a property is equal to the price recently paid for similar properties.

**Competing offers:** Offers to purchase that have been made by two buyers at the same time.

**Completion date:** The date on which a buyer becomes the registered owner of the property in exchange for paying the purchase price in trust to the seller's lawyer or notary.

**Condition precedents:** Conditions that must be met in order for a contract to be fulfilled.

**Condominium:** See *strata title ownership*.

**Condominium mortgage:** A mortgage in which the buyer of a condominium unit receives legal title to the unit he or she is purchasing, as well as an undivided interest in the common area.

**Contingency fund:** A fund of money held in reserve by a strata corporation to pay for emergency repairs or other unforeseen events.

**Contract of purchase and sale:** A statement of an agreement's terms and conditions, recorded in legal form.

**Conventional mortgage loan:** A mortgage loan that allows borrowing an amount equal to up to 75 percent of the purchase price or the appraised value of the property, whichever is less.

**Conveyancer:** The lawyer or notary who completes the transfer and register of title (the conveyancing) to the new owner.

**Co-operative:** A type of ownership in which buyers purchase shares in the company that owns a property; they become co-owners.

**Co-ownership:** Ownership by more than one person.

**Counter-offer:** An alternative offer made by either party in response to an offer.

**Curable defects:** Property deficiencies that can easily be remedied or fixed.

**Deposit:** An amount of money given with an offer to purchase to show that the offer is in earnest.

**Detached home:** A home that stands alone without being attached to another building.

**Down payment:** An initial partial payment made when a property is purchased.

**Duplex:** A building containing two separate residences, either side by side or one on top of the other. (See also *semi-detached*.)

**Easement:** A defined area of a private property over which certain legal rights are given to another, usually adjacent, property (commonly for access, utility, or encroachment purposes).

**Empty nesters:** People whose children have left home or who have retired.

**Exclusion list:** A list of items that are not included in the purchase price.

**Exclusive listing:** An agreement in which a seller gives one agent or agency the authority to offer a property for sale, lease, or exchange during a specific time period. The seller agrees to pay the listing agent a commission, even if the seller eventually sells the property him- or herself.

**Fee simple:** Private ownership of real estate in which the owner has the right to control, use, and transfer the property at will.

**Fixed closing costs:** A fixed amount of money to be paid on closing.

**Fixed rate mortgage:** A mortgage contract that is written for terms ranging from six months to ten years. Penalties may be triggered if the borrower wishes to end the contract before the term expires (early repayment).

**Fixture:** An item in a building, or on land, that is considered part of the property; it is usually affixed to the property by a nail, screw, or something similar.

**Flipping:** This term refers to a property that is bought for the sole purpose of reselling it quickly for a profit.

**Flood plain:** A lowland area, whether dyked, floodproofed, or unprotected, which is at an elevation susceptible to flooding.

**For Sale by Owner (FSBO):** A private sale between a seller and buyer, done without third parties (i.e., real estate agents) acting as intermediaries, or with an agent acting on behalf of the buyer only.

**Form "B" or estoppel certificate:** A document that indicates how much money is in a strata corporation's contingency fund for emergencies.

**Fractional ownership:** Fractional ownership gives you a deeded share (equity) in a vacation residence and the right to use it a certain amount of time per year (usually 4 to 12 weeks). Fractional properties are often located in vacation resorts, come fully furnished, and have maintenance and upkeep handled by a property management company for an annual fee.

**Freehold:** Ownership of a property, with full use and control of the land and the buildings on it.

**Genuine consent:** Knowledge that the buyers understand what they are buying and are aware of everything that could affect their title if they buy a property.

**Gross debt service ratio:** A test of a borrower's ability to repay a loan that allows the borrower no more than 32 percent of gross monthly income (before deductions) to make monthly housing payments.

**High-ratio loan:** A loan that allows the buyer to borrow more than 75 percent of the purchase price or the appraised value of the property, whichever is less.

**Home stagers:** Companies that prepare homes for showing during open houses.

**Hot sheet:** A list of properties that have just been listed for sale through the Multiple Listing Service (MLS); although this list is eventually shown to the public, realtors have early access to this information, which gives them a "window of opportunity" of about three to five days, including weekends and holidays.

**Incurable defects:** Property defects that are too difficult or too expensive to fix, such as structural or foundational defects.

**Investment property:** A property that the owner rents out to one or more tenants in order to make money.

**Joint tenancy:** A type of ownership in which property is co-owned, common among those purchasing with a spouse or partner. If one party dies, the entire ownership automatically transfers to the survivor, without having to go through probate.

**Land title search:** A search carried out to discover who is registered as the current owner of the property and if any registered mortgages, easements, restrictive covenants, or rights-of-way may affect the use or value of the property in a positive or negative way.

**Leasehold:** Holding a property by lease for a defined period of time. The lessee owns the buildings and improvements but not the land.

**Letter of commitment:** A letter from a lending institution stating how much it is willing to lend, at what rate, and on which terms.

**Listing agent:** A real estate licensee hired by a seller to help sell property; an agency relationship is created in which the seller becomes the principal and the licensee becomes the agent of the seller.

**Listing agreement:** A contract that sets out in writing the arrangement between a seller and a real estate agent.

**Lowball offer:** An offer that is substantially lower than the price the seller is asking.

**Maintenance fees:** Strata property fees that include the costs of insurance, management fees, and the upkeep of common property.

**Manufactured home:** A factory-built residential structure, typically designed with wheels so that it can be moved from one place to another. It is often placed on a rented space called a "pad" in a manufactured-home park. Also known as a mobile home or a prefab.

**Market value:** The amount a home is worth in the current market, compared to other houses for sale or recently sold.

**Mortgage:** An agreement to lend money to finance the purchase of property; the property is held as security for the loan.

**Mortgage application fee:** A type of insurance required on all mortgage loans that exceed 75 percent of the appraised property value; its purpose is to ensure that a lender will not lose any money if the borrower cannot make mortgage payments and if the value of the property is not sufficient to repay the borrower's mortgage debt.

**Mortgage default insurance:** Insurance that ensures that if you default on your mortgage, the lender will be paid by the insurer, who is either the CMHC or a private company.

**Multiple Listing Service (MLS):** A listing of properties for sale that is available to all real estate agents who are members of their local real estate board.

**Multiple offers:** Offers made by more than two parties at the same time.

**Municipal assessment:** A municipality's assessment of the value of a property and the amount of property taxes payable for the year.

**Named perils policy:** A named perils policy offers protection only for those perils listed in the insurance policy, for example, fire and lightning.

**Notary:** A person who can perform certain legal duties, such as filing legal forms, but who is not a lawyer.

**Open house:** An event in which a seller opens his or her house to real estate agents and the general public so that potential buyers can come in and look at it.

**Open listing:** A relatively loose verbal agreement in which the seller gives one or more real estate agencies the authority to find a buyer for a property.

**Open mortgage:** A mortgage in which the borrower can repay a loan, in part or in full, at any time without penalty.

**Party wall:** The wall shared by two halves of a duplex or two units in a row house or apartment.

**Portable mortgage:** A mortgage loan that can be transferred to another property when a person decides to sell the existing property and buy a new one.

**Possession date:** The date on which the buyer takes physical possession of a property.

**Principal:** In a purchase situation, the buyer is the principal of the agent. In a seller situation, the seller is the principal of the agent.

**Prefab home:** This can include cabins, cottages, or single-family dwellings that are pre-assembled to some degree before they are delivered to a property.

**Pre-qualification:** A buyer obtains approval from a bank that it will lend him a certain amount of money for a mortgage before the buyer places an offer on a home.

**Pre-termination charges:** A penalty the borrower is charged by a lender if the borrower pays off a mortgage before the actual termination date.

**Private sale:** See *For Sale by Owner*.

**Property condition disclosure statement** (PCDS): A statement, signed by the seller, that provides a history and description of the condition of the property, including details of environmental, structural, and mechanical issues and water, sewage, plumbing, and renovation information. Also known as a disclosure statement.

**Property taxes:** Taxes paid by the registered owner of a property to a municipality.

**Real estate agent:** A person who assists in buying or selling real estate. Also known as an agent.

**Replacement cost:** For an older house, the cost of replacing it with a modern equivalent.

**Restrictive covenant:** A legal obligation imposed on a deed by the seller that requires the buyer to do or refrain from doing certain things on the property.

**Right-of-way:** The right to pass over property owned by another party.

**Riparian rights:** An owner's right in land that borders on or includes a stream, river, or lake. These rights include access to and use of the water.

**Semi-detached:** A housing unit that shares only one wall with an adjoining unit.

**Special assessment:** An assessment generally rendered by a condominium corporation to individual unit holders to pay for major improvements to a complex, such as to fix a roof or repair a parking garage, which may be extraordinary expenses that were not budgeted for and which cannot be fully covered by the monies in the contingency fund.

**Stakeholder:** A stakeholder is a consideration for an offer with a monetary value. It can be as little as one dollar and is given with the offer to show intention.

**Strata title ownership:** A type of housing ownership in which buyers not only own a unit, but share ownership of common areas such as hallways, garages, and elevators.

**Subject clauses:** See *condition precedents*.

**Survey certificate:** A certificate showing that a survey has been conducted to formally establish the boundaries of a property, to ensure that all buildings are within those boundaries, and to ensure that a house is not encroaching on other properties.

**Tenancy in common:** A form of co-ownership in which each owner may or may not have the same amount of shares or rights. As a result, one party may sell his or her share without the permission of others.

**Term:** The period of time in which a mortgage is written, ranging from six months to ten years.

**Timeshare:** Co-ownership of a vacation property in a resort that allows you a specified number of weeks' use each year in perpetuity.

**Title insurance:** A one-time premium that insures against defects in title that may otherwise prevent a transaction from closing or that may arise after the property is purchased.

**Title search:** A search carried out to discover who is registered as the current owner of the property and if any registered mortgages, easements, restrictive covenants, or rights-of-way may affect the use or value of the property in a positive or negative way.

**Total debt service ratio:** The ability to repay a loan, based on assets, liabilities, earnings, employment history, and past record of repaying loans.

**Townhouse:** One of a row of adjoined homes, usually all of a similar style.

**Transaction levy:** Unique to Ontario, a fee required to be paid to the Lawyers' Professional Indemnity Company (owned by the Law Society of Upper Canada) on some title-insured transactions.

**Transfer document:** The document that transfers title to a property from the seller to the buyer.

**Transfer taxes:** Sometimes known as property transfer taxes, transfer taxes are taxes paid when real property is transferred from one owner to the next. Some provinces provide first-time homebuyers with a break on transfer taxes related to the property purchase.

**Vendor take-back (VTB) mortgage:** A mortgage that allows home-buyers a chance to purchase a property with the help of the seller, who lends them a portion of the purchase price.

**Zoning:** Local government specifications regarding the types of buildings that may be built on particular properties and how those buildings may be used; for example, as single- or multi-family residential units, as duplexes, or as commercial or industrial structures.